THE BARMAID,

THE BEAN COUNTER,

AND THE BUNGEE JUMPER

A COLLECTION OF SHORT STORIES AND POETRY BY PEBBLES, THE THUNDERBIRD WRITERS' GROUP

THE BARMAID,
THE BEAN COUNTER,
AND THE BUNGEE JUMPER

A COLLECTION OF SHORT STORIES
AND POETRY BY PEBBLES,
THE THUNDERBIRD WRITERS' GROUP

ISBN # 0-9676848-5-4
Published by Thunderbird Publishing
P O Box 22830
Carmel, CA 93922

Cover art by Dan Koffman
Back cover design: Ken Jones
Book design: Marnie Sperry
Introduction by May Waldroup
Editing: Marnie Sperry, Walter Gourlay

The Pebbles Writers Group
dedicates this book with great affection
to May, our dear PMH,
with many thanks for her
superb leadership, hard work,
and warm friendship.

TABLE OF CONTENTS

TABLE OF CONTENTS

INTRODUCTION

Four years have passed since we published "Pebbles", our first collection of short stories and poems.

Since then, several things have changed.

We still meet twice a month on Thursdays at the Thunderbird Bookshop but our group has grown, even though some of our original members have left for other parts of the world. New members bring new talent and new ideas, especially when they have come from other writing groups who have a different modus operandi than ours.

The diversity of PEBBLES is seen even further in "Pocket Pieces" in this book, one of our writing exercises in which the group was given one subject about which to write. Imaginations soared, as each of our "pockets" contained amazingly diverse items.

I wish you could be an unseen guest at our bi-monthly meetings when we listen to and critique our writings. It would give you a good idea of how a book like ours comes to fruition and you would notice the change that has come about, not only because of the new members but because we have become more perceptive and are willing (albeit kicking and screaming) to subject our writing to group critiquing. I think that was the hardest hurdle we had to overcome...and yet like a cold shower, it invigorates us.

Criticism and praise is productive when a group has trust amongst its members. We have that trust and the will to improve our writing has root in this fertile soil.

We owe a debt to Elliot Rachowitz-Roberts who carefully combed through the first incarnation of this book. He gave us good counsel and moved us on to where he would probably not recognize this presentation.

In the past four years, e-mail has played a considerable part in the daily dialogue amongst our members. Martin Dodd, a computer/e-mail wizard, took it upon himself to keep us on a tight tether once we set a timetable for publishing this volume. With a gentle e-mail whip, he marshaled us into deadline shape. A large debt of appreciation for his gentle conscientiousness is hereby paid in some small measure.

Marnie Sperry was the moving spirit in getting "Pebbles" published. She was an early Internet "diva" and saw us through all the hurdles of self-publishing. She has done it again with infinite patience, and earns a resounding round of applause from us all.

Here then is our latest, *The Barmaid, The Bean Counter and The Bungee Jumper*. We have enjoyed the writing, may you enjoy the reading.

MAY WALDROUP

THE BARMAID,

THE BEAN COUNTER,

AND THE BUNGEE JUMPER

A COLLECTION OF SHORT STORIES
AND POETRY BY PEBBLES,
THE THUNDERBIRD WRITERS' GROUP

THE BARMAID, THE BEAN COUNTER, AND THE BUNGEE JUMPER

PETER HOSS

Once upon a time in the far away city of Seattle there lived a fair young barmaid with blonde hair, ruddy cheeks and a sunny smile. She was attractive and hard working, but she became obsessed with a notion so wild and crazy that she did not want to talk to anyone about it. She wanted to bungee jump off the Space Needle. She could not get the idea out of her mind. She thought of it day after day. She would dream about it in her gloomy studio apartment under the gloomy wintry skies of Seattle. She did not know how to bungee jump or where to learn. She longed to meet a handsome bungee jumper who would teach her.

There also lived in the same city a young man who had a steady, good paying job with good benefits as a bean counter. However, the job was boring and he longed for adventure. He did not know what kind of adventure he wanted, and he was afraid to leave his steady job with good benefits.

One day the fair young barmaid saw an ad for a job in the restaurant atop the Space Needle. She applied because it would be one step closer to her dream. She was accepted because she was attractive, hard working and had good references.

The bean counter, shy and terrified of asking girls for dates (so he had few dates) enjoyed going to the Space Needle for a drink. He would sometimes see the fair barmaid and think of asking for a date, but his shyness would always overcome

1

him and he would go to his small gloomy studio apartment in a melancholy mood and return to his dreams of adventure and then go back to his bean counting job the next day.

The fair barmaid finally decided she had to share her dream with someone, so she told another barmaid about it. The shy bean counter was having a drink, overheard the conversation, and thought that if he could learn to bungee jump, he could ask the fair barmaid if she would go bungee jumping with him and she would probably accept. He went home more excited than he had been in a long time and looked up bungee jumping on the Internet. Lo and behold, he found a bungee jumping school in Seattle. He was elated. He immediately called the bungee jumping school and made an appointment.

It was the first call the bungee jumping instructor had received in a week. His bungee jumping business was failing. No one seemed interested. He would go home each night to a gloomy studio apartment, eat macaroni and cheese, and dream of having a steady job with good benefits.

The shy bean counter took his first lesson. The financially distressed bungee jumping instructor was amazed. He said he had never seen anyone with so much natural talent. He encouraged the shy bean counter to continue the lessons. The shy bean counter did so. He could afford the lessons because he had a steady job with good benefits. Within three weeks, the shy bean counter had surpassed the skills of his instructor and was teaching *him* new tricks.

The shy bean counter was now ready to ask the fair barmaid to go bungee jumping with him. He steeled his nerves and asked her. Her heart fluttered and she was ecstatic. This was her dream come true. This was the man of her dreams, her Prince Charming. She noticed that he was handsome. He taught her bungee jumping and she excelled in it also. The financially distressed bungee jumping instructor opined that he had never seen two people so gifted, but they were his only customers. His business was still failing, and he was really tired of eating macaroni and cheese. He still longed for a steady job with good benefits.

2

The fair barmaid and the shy bean counter fell madly in love. She shared with him her dream to bungee jump off the Space Needle. He said he wanted to make it his dream also. He said he would design the world's longest bungee cord so they could do it together. It would be a bungee cord made for two. He worked hard at it and found the best craftsmen to make the bungee cord. He could afford this because he had a steady job with good benefits.

The financially distressed bungee jumping instructor continued to brood about his failing business over his nightly macaroni and cheese. The only thing that could save it, he thought, would be a gigantic publicity stunt that would call attention and awaken interest in bungee jumping, but he did not know how to go about it and he had no money.

Finally the world's longest bungee jumping cord and the first and only bungee jumping cord made for two was completed. The shy bean counter and the fair barmaid decided to install it secretly in the Space Needle and test it secretly before asking official permission. They were not sure how to go about this, since it is difficult to test such an operation in secret.

One night while the fair barmaid was on duty and the shy bean counter was having a drink, a robber wearing a ski mask walked into the restaurant atop the Space Needle, demanded all the cash in the till and severed all the telephone lines so no one could call to apprehend him below when he got off the elevator. The fair barmaid and the shy bean counter knew what to do. In a flash they were on the bungee cord for two and were at the bottom of the Space Needle before the elevator arrived. "Hold the cord," the shy bean counter said to the fair barmaid. When the elevator arrived, the shy bean counter overpowered the robber, retrieved the money and tied the robber to the bungee cord all in one quick motion. "Let go," he said to the fair barmaid. She did, and the robber was catapulted to the top of the Space Needle, where he lay dazed and could not comprehend what had happened. He was apprehended and punished appropriately for his evil deed.

The fair barmaid and the shy bean counter were instant heroes. Their heroic feat was front-page news. Everyone wanted to learn bungee jumping. The police and the army wanted to train an elite bungee jumping corps. The financially distressed bungee jumper offered jobs to the shy bean counter and fair barmaid, but he could not pay benefits. Besides, the shy bean counter and the fair barmaid wanted to own their own business, to satisfy their dreams for a lifelong adventure together. The financially distressed bungee jumping instructor knew he could not compete with instant heroes, and besides they were better bungee jumpers than he was. All he wanted was a steady job with good benefits. The shy bean counter had an idea.

He suggested to the financially distressed bungee jumping instructor, "If I quit my job to start this business, I will need a replacement. Perhaps I could teach you bean counting and you could take my job. It is a steady job with good benefits."

"Would you do that for me?" asked the financially distressed bungee jumping instructor, a great weight falling from his shoulders.

"It is the least I could do," said the shy bean counter. "After all, you taught me bungee jumping. I owe it all to you."

The shy bean counter taught bean counting to the financially distressed bungee jumping instructor. He observed that he had never seen anyone with such a natural talent for bean counting. The financially distressed bungee jumping instructor soon became better than the shy bean counter had ever been.

The owner of the bean business was delighted and said to the financially distressed bungee jumping instructor, "As long as you want, you have a steady job with this company, with good benefits."

The shy bean counter and the fair barmaid were married. They went bungee jumping every day and never tired of it. Their business prospered, and they moved out of their gloomy studio apartments into a beautiful home on Queen

Anne Hill with a spectacular view of Elliott Bay and the Olympic Mountains. They raised a brood of little bungee jumpers.

The financially distressed bungee jumping instructor never ate macaroni and cheese again and moved out of his gloomy studio apartment into a home next door to the shy bean counter and the fair barmaid. He married a co-worker at the bean company who also had a steady job with good benefits. They raised a brood of little bean counters.

They all lived happily ever after.

THE DEAD WOMAN'S EARRINGS
LYNDA SPERRY JARDINE

I think of her each time I pin to my ears
Coral and silver earrings
Long desired, finally possessed.
Imagination recalls the artisan
Seated, shoulders and back hunched
Over her table, body and being intent
Within the stark aura of her work light
The dim room beyond
Darkened more in contrast.
Wood smoke's musty perfume
Escapes from dying embers
In a cooling wood stove.
Coffee is cold in its cup.
In winter's evening chill
Arthritis slows her fingers and hands.

Within this dominion of creativity
Encircled in light
She spends her essence
On polished stone and silver
Ignores winter's aches
Unaware of a signal within
Sending a message to her brain.
Her eyes close.

A LETTER – 1990

MAY WALDROUP

She held the letter in her hand. A letter for her? Yes, it clearly said *Frau Anneke Paulson, 24 Guttinger Strasse, Kirken/Dresden Deutschland.* Imagine—a letter for her! It had been years since she had received a handwritten letter.

She turned it over and read the return address: *Brigitte Paulson, Gunther Str. 15, Stuttgart, Deutschland.* Slowly she turned the letter over and over again. Brigitte Paulson, the wife of her late husband's brother, still alive in what had always been West Germany in her mind. It had been almost fifty years since they had last heard from each other and that had been...best not to remember that.

It was a heavy letter. The mailman had just given it to her as she was hanging her sparse laundry on the line outside her door. He had made her sign her name in a registry book. *"Einschreiben"* was written in bold letters on the envelope, not in the same penmanship as the address, probably by someone at the post office who collected the extra fee for a registered letter.

She put the last clothespin into the pocket of her apron and slowly, painfully entered the old, shabby apartment house.

Her one room living quarter was not bad, at least it was on the ground floor. She could no longer walk up the dark stairs that led to the larger apartments above her. Also, hers was a good-sized room with running water, and she had fashioned a little kitchen for herself. The bathroom was at the end of the hallway and was shared with a family living across from her.

She had managed reasonably well all these years. The modest pension that she collected kept her fed. Potatoes were cheap; bread and cabbage were cheap as well. Her fellow apartment dwellers were greeted with the strong smell of cabbage almost every day as they climbed the stairs to their own modest apartments. She had not gained weight over the years, and in fact her World War II clothes still fit her – at least those that had survived. They had been mended and patched many times – no one cared what anyone looked like those days. Those days were long gone.

She opened the door to her room and slowly sat down in her chair near the window. A small candle in a shallow dish stood on the table beside her. Automatically she lit it, as was her wont at the end of every day when dusk set in.

She looked at the letter again, reluctantly picked up her darning scissors and carefully cut one of the seams of the envelope. Then she drew out the pages. They were tightly folded, closed around something. Her old arthritic fingers slowly loosened the edges and there, where other letters held nothing but words, was a bill, a bill of money, one hundred marks; and there was more, there were ten of these bills, one thousand *Deutschmark*, an absolute fortune! Her hands trembled as she placed the money carefully on the table. This was overwhelming. "*Lieber Gott, wie ist das moglich?*" But God was not speaking to her just now.

She put her hand over her eyes, overcome by this event. All these years there had been silence between them, silence that would go to the grave with the two sisters-in-law, silence that was born out of all-too-human emotions, love and hate, love for one man, hate for the woman who should not have loved her man. Tears of agony, tears of remembrance fell on the letter.

With a sigh, she unfolded the two pages. "*Meine liebe Anneke.*" "*Liebe?*" "Dear?" They had not been dear to each other for fifty years. "You will be surprised to hear from me after all these years. I enquired at the town hall and found that you were still registered as living and they found me

8

your last known address. Dear Anneke, before I say anything else, I wish to beg for your forgiveness for the pain I have brought into your life all these years."

Anneke closed her eyes. The letter dropped into her lap as she wiped her eyes. Then the tears were welling up again. Yes, all these years...

When Walter's brother died, he went to comfort the widow, and together they had grieved. It had been a tragic accident and Brigitte had been left with two little boys. Walter did what he could for her and her children but she clung onto him as though he was her life raft. Over the years she begged for his presence, his guidance with the boys, and he was always there for her. The boys grew up thinking of him as their father. Then the war ended and a wall, a political and physical wall, separated East and West Germany. Walter, in a last effort, crossed over into Berlin and found Brigitte, leaving Anneke behind.

"My dear Anneke, Walter helped me and the boys but he never could forget what he did to you. As he grew older he became more morose, he hardly spoke to me. He would sit in his chair by the window and look out towards the East. He died last year a sad and silent man. He left all his savings to you. He had come to realize that he loved you, and only you."

Anneke was sobbing, loud, heart-wrenching sobs came from her innermost soul. Finally, finally there was a message from the man she had loved for so long and who could no longer speak for himself.

He had loved her after all.

Through her tears she read the last paragraph.

"*Ich habe eine Wohnung fur dich*--your financial future is secure and if you come and live in the house I have for you, I can try to make your life one of comfort. I offer you my deepest regret and my love to mend the past."

A loud cry of agony escaped from Anneke.

* * *

She held the key in her hand. The old lace curtains had

9

been drawn in her room, the water turned off, the hotplate wiped and stored. The clothespins bulged in the pocket of her apron, which hung on a knob near her sink. She had stopped cooking cabbage and the air near the door was fresh and clear.

She turned around and looked at her little world, the world of the past fifty years. In her hand was a small satchel with the best clothes she owned.

The little candle she had lit when she first got Brigitte's letter still rested on the table. She would just light it again to say good-bye to the life she had led – alone and lonely, knowing that Walter was in the arms of her sister-in-law.

She struck a match and the little wick caught fire and slowly grew. Her handbag rested on her knobby knees, it was as old and wrinkled as she felt. In it were her ticket and the money that would lead her to a brighter, less burdensome future.

Slowly she looked around the room. Yes, it had been her refuge, her small comfort in a hard and lonely life.

Everything was in order – the dishes clean, the apron washed, her bed made up, her past well ordered. Her future awaited her...

As she looked around the room in the candlelight, a panorama of her past life, her love, her sorrow passed before her eyes, her soul...

"No," she thought – "*No.*"

"NO."

Slowly she opened her bag and took out her train ticket. Behind it was the money.

"**NO!**" she said loudly.

She took the ticket and with a trembling hand held it to the flame of the candle – then she took a one hundred *Deutschmark* bill--and the next, and the next--until the ashes around the candle were the ashes of her past.

After a while she got up, slowly opened her small satchel, and unpacked.

THE STORYTELLER
MARTIN DODD

Her wrinkled face shows gathered abundance,
Each line a cut from Time's sure scythe.
She gleans wisdom grains from the harvest
And spins her tales as straw to gold.
A rose with fading petals, she shares
The hugging joy of the spring bud's dream,
Sweet fragrant memories of summer's bloom,
Adding her unique scent to life's potpourri.
Her stories intend the path of progeny,
Telling of laughter and tears,
Of promise in the journey,
Suggesting her influence in destiny.
    In telling, she forges a link in the chain
    And leaves a footprint of her passing.

VISITATION

ILLIA THOMPSON

Wingspans create
umbrella shadows.
Two Canadian Geese
fly over the pool

honk lofty presence
reverse flight pattern
to include an early
morning swim.

They splash about
in their sanctuary,
dip pale orange beaks
in and out of cool liquid.

Bodies beautified
by cleansing water,
they note location
on bird's eye map.

Only upon viewing
themselves in the
plate glass window
do they fly away.

A spot already
occupied by such
a handsome couple,
no longer theirs.

THE STORM

GEORGIA A. HUBLEY

The wind hurled spring rain against the windshield. Even the high-speed wipers were no match for the downpour. Jenny gripped the steering wheel as visibility worsened. It'd been miles since she'd seen another car on the winding two-lane road. She wondered if the Overland Bridge was out up ahead, and pulled over to the shoulder to wait out the storm.

She shivered as the rain hammered the roof of her white sedan. Unbuckling her seatbelt, she reached for her khaki raincoat on the empty passenger's seat. Loud thunder clamored overhead, startling her as she struggled into the raincoat, and her hand bumped the rear view mirror. While straightening the mirror, she slipped her left arm into the other sleeve. As she fastened the top two buttons of the raincoat, she caught a glimpse of a small beam of light, possibly a flashlight in the distance. Quickly, she turned around and looked out of the back window, wondering if someone else was stranded in the storm. The light was gone. Maybe her eyes were playing tricks, but she trembled as the eeriness swept over her, wondering how long she'd be stranded in the car. Perhaps if she turned on the radio, there'd be news about the weather, but all she heard was static, havoc caused by the storm. All attempts to use her cell phone were futile.

Lightning continued to zigzag across the sky. The storm was not subsiding. As another flash of lightning lit up the road, she glanced behind her. Was someone standing in the middle of the road? Her vision was blurred as the wind and rain continued to pummel her car. Condensation was beginning

13

to fill in the back window; again she could see a tiny beam of light in the distance. Mesmerized, she watched as the light moved closer and closer. It came from a dark figure stumbling along the shoulder of the road, heading toward her car. The car doors were locked, but there was no place to hide. Engulfed in fear, her heart pulsating in her ears, her whole body shaking, she prepared for the worst. Remembering the heavy-duty black flashlight she kept underneath the driver's seat, she placed it on her lap.

Unaware the dark figure had approached the driver's side of the car, in fright she jolted out of her seat, hitting her head on the sunroof when the stranger used a large silver flashlight to bang on her car window. Lightning struck somewhere in the distance, providing enough light to learn the dark figure's identity. Relieved, she pressed her nose against the cold window.

"Tom Gentry, is that you?" Jenny yelled, competing with the thunder and wind. "You're drenched. Why are you walking in weather like this?"

"I'm searching for Luke!" he shouted.

Forgetting the storm for a moment, she lowered her window slightly. "Tom, get in the car, we'll wait out the storm together. I'll help you look for Luke."

Quickly Tom opened the car door and hurled himself into the passenger's seat; the rain from his black rubberized rain gear saturated the inside of the car. "Thanks, Jenny. I'm sorry I've made everything sopping wet."

"Tom, it doesn't matter. We'll all dry out." As Tom removed his soaked black hat, she couldn't help but notice he seemed different than the last time she'd seen him. He looked old and tired, but of course he must be exhausted from walking so far in the wind and rain. She remembered how much he loved his dog Luke, a beautiful German shepherd.

Tom interrupted her thoughts. "Luke is such a good dog, my faithful companion. A dog is man's best friend, that's my Luke. He's getting up there. He's fifteen, and thunder and lightning bother him. That's why he ran off the way he did."

"Won't he come back home once the storm is over?" asked Jenny.

"His sight isn't what it used to be. Last time there was a storm he was so scared, he hid under the Overland Bridge up ahead until I came looking for him," explained Tom. "By the way, your Aunt Ella and Uncle Bill are sure looking forward to your visit. I saw them Friday morning on the way to the grocery store. They told everyone they met that you were coming into town, taking a detour from your annual stockholders' meeting in the city."

Jenny laughed. "Tom, how long have you and Luke lived next door to Aunt Ella and Uncle Bill?" she asked.

"I reckon about fifty years. Your Aunt Ella and Uncle Bill were newlyweds when they moved into the old homestead that belonged to your aunt's family. The house stood empty for the longest time. The lawyer handling the estate hired me to keep an eye on the place since I was living next door with my mother, working at the Starlight movie theatre, going to school and taking care of her and all. That's why I never married. A confirmed bachelor for seventy years, guess I stopped looking. Never found anyone who'd put up with my mother and me. 'Course she suffered so, had to have nurses come in to take care of her the last year of her life. She's been gone twenty years now."

As Tom digressed, Jenny dialed her cell phone, to no avail. "No luck. I was trying to reach Aunt Ella and Uncle Bill."

"They know you're coming," Tom said. "I think the storm is letting up. The wind has died down. I'll take a look outside."

Jenny lowered her window as Tom circled her sedan. "I'm sinking into the mud as I walk around out here. You're in a bit of trouble; your tires have sunk into the mud. Try starting your car so I can see if you have any traction."

As he predicted, the tires spun around and around, digging deeper into the shoulder of the road. "Stop! Stop!" shouted Tom.

Tired and frustrated, all Jenny wanted was a nice hot

15

bath and one of Aunt Ella's home-cooked meals. Unable to hide her exasperation, she yelled, "Tom, what can I do? It's late, my phone doesn't work, and it is too far to walk to Aunt Ella and Uncle Bill's place!" Then she remembered Luke. "Maybe we can walk back to where you parked your car. I can leave my car here until morning. You can take me home after we find Luke."

"No, I have an idea. You should be heading to your aunt and uncle's, not out here with me all night searching for Luke. Start your engine and step down hard on the gas. I'll give you a push."

Before she could protest, Tom was behind her car, shouting, "Go, when I say Go!" As she stepped on the gas, she was astonished that her car suddenly lurched forward and was back on the road. Tooting her horn to thank him, she looked in the rear view mirror, and Tom bid her farewell by waving the flashlight over his head. A sweet old man, she thought. Tomorrow she'd do something special for him.

Without incident, Jenny drove the quarter of a mile to Vandalia, home of Aunt Ella and Uncle Bill and Tom Gentry. The countryside seemed to have weathered the severity of the storm. Luckily, no fallen trees or debris blocked the road; even the Overland Bridge was safe to cross. Pleased to be at her destination at last, she saw Uncle Bill peering through the sheer curtains at the front window. She set the parking brake and reached for her suitcase in the back seat, and spotted Tom's drenched black hat on the floor. She'd definitely see Tom tomorrow.

Jenny wrestled with her suitcase. "What's going on?" she asked herself. Was it her imagination, or was the tan canvas suitcase heavier than when she put it in the back seat? Her stomach rumbled, reminding her it'd been at least ten hours since breakfast. No wonder she'd lost her strength, she thought, knowing the suitcase was more than she could manage on an empty stomach. After supper, she'd have Uncle Bill help her retrieve the suitcase.

The aroma of Aunt Ella's pot roast filled her nostrils as Uncle Bill opened the front door and gave her a big hug.

"We were worried you were stranded. Thought maybe the Overland Bridge washed out again and you had to go miles out of your way to get here."

"Oh, the Overland Bridge is just fine, but there was such a heavy downpour and strong winds, I couldn't see the road. Just before I reached the bridge, I had to pull off to the shoulder and wait it out. But Tom Gentry was good company, he was out in the storm looking for Luke. After the rain stopped, Tom discovered my tires had sunk into the mud and he pushed me out. I sure owe him a heap of thanks. Tomorrow I must do something special for him."

Frowning, Uncle Bill shook his head and replied, "Jenny, it was dark, storming real bad, you didn't see Tom tonight."

"But I did see him," Jenny insisted. "Tom said that you and..."

Aunt Ella interrupted, "Last Friday, Tom and Luke were walking on the Overland Bridge. A hit and run, and in broad daylight too. Killed them instantly. Tom's funeral is tomorrow morning. I hope you can come with us."

Jenny nodded. Stunned by the news, she was speechless until she remembered the wet black hat in the back of her car. "Uncle Bill, could you help me bring in my suitcase?" she asked.

Silently, they walked to her car. Jenny opened the left rear door and was astounded by what she saw. Her tan canvas suitcase and the entire back seat were dripping wet. The black hat was gone. Uncle Bill broke the silence. "Hey, everything's soaked back here. During the storm, I reckon you forgot to roll up your back window."

JOYFUL ABANDON
HELEN OLSON

They burst upon the spacious beach
As the furred, free spirits they are.
Legs and tails, snouts and ears
Jet amidst the dancing wind
Flitting, flying, gliding in joyful motion.

So much play to be had
With 'he' and 'she' of like spirit,
Of like canine kind.
Yet too the tantalizing distraction
Of a potentially friendly human,
The two-legged beings with loving pats
And curious toys.

With winged feet they glide
First one way, then swiftly another
Over the sand, into the surf
Chasing each other
Following their spirits
Panting smiles
And nothing but joyful abandon.

THE HAINT IN THE HILLS

PATRICIA MATUSZEWSKI

"You planning to camp in the Santa Lucias? Not too many people who grew up in Big Sur do that. I never will again," he said, pulling the sleeve of his work shirt up to the elbow and, with a gesture, indicating the gouges on his arm that went all the way up it to his scarred face. "I don't exactly know, but what I think is, I think my Gramma's haint got me. You never heard of a haint? Well, if you're set on going into the mountains, I better tell you what she told me. Wish I'd believed her then."

It was in the 1860's or thereabouts, a cold night, the kind we call a three dog night 'cause that's how many dogs you need in bed with you to keep warm. Rand Millins whistled up his hound dog, grabbed one of his fine jugs of 'shine, and set off to visit Joe Jeffrey in his shack up Palo Colorado. Like always, they sat around the potbelly stove in the kitchen, drinking, spitting tobacco on the stovetop, telling lies and boasting.

"Well," said Rand, "I gotta tell ya. That hound of mine is the best cat dog I ever seen. Treed ten so far. Got no fear. No siree, no fear. I've got me a job on the Corona Ranch getting rid of mountain lions, pays real good."

Joe was puzzling out how to top this when all hell broke loose – scrabbling paws and claws punctuated by falling milk cans, tools, a chair falling over, then ferocious barking, yowling, growling, and spitting. By the time the men sorted out their legs and got them working well enough to stumble outside, all they could see was the hound's disappearing rear with the scrawny mean, stray cat that claimed the porch in pursuit. *They swore that when that cat caught up to that hound they just seemed to melt together, shape shift, and a new animal, huge and fierce, formed and grew. It was solid, yet they could see right through it, see the moon, the hills, the forest where they should never have been. Unless what they were seeing was a haint.*

The beast turned glowing yellow eyes on them, snarled, and raised its head to the strange white light of the full moon. It screamed like a mountain lion. It howled like a wolf. It vanished without moving. That scream-howl will make your blood run cold. You can still hear it on cold clear nights in the darkest valleys and on the highest ridges of the Santa Lucias. It's on those nights that local folk stay inside. In the morning they know they'll find paw prints, a mountain lion's in front, a wolf's in the rear. And they'll find sheep or cows or horses, their throats ripped open. Sometimes they find people.

"This is what my grandma told me but I didn't believe her. My buddies and me went out drinking one of those cold bright nights. I'm the only one came back.

"Well, I see you want to get on your way. I guess you think I'm telling you a tall tale because you're new here. You're still going into those mountains, aren't you? I'm sorry. Real sorry." He turned to walk away, his eyes gleaming wild and yellow, his lips turning up in a snarl.

THE RETURN OF THE PRINCESS OF PERIODICALS: A CARMEL FAIRYTALE

JOY WARE

Once upon a time in the literary principality of Carmel-by-the-Sea, there lived the widowed Sire of Scripts and his only daughter, Marianna. Daily they walked the curving shoreline from 13th Street to the bluffs of Pebble Beach and back. Against the backdrop of roiling seas, and gray skies, or water blue and still as a mill pond, the Sire of Scripts would enchant his lanky, golden-haired princess with tales of kings who overcame intrigues, and knights on white horses who rescued damsels in distress. In the late afternoon, an artist or writer would drop by for tea and discuss whatever work was in progress. The princess and her sire shared *The Man in the Iron Mask*, *The Three Musketeers*, *The Count of Monte Cristo*, and all of Jane Austen. The Sire and Princess applauded the players, and occasionally graced the stage of the Golden Bough Circle Theater themselves. Thus Princess Marianna's life was steeped in Carmel's haven for those drawn to the power of words—oral, written, true, or purely fiction.

Over time, Marianna's curiosity beckoned her to places well beyond the principality of Carmel-by-the-Sea. It was therefore no surprise when she fell completely under the sway of the cosmopolitan manners of a vacationing diplomat whose post was in Salzburg. The Sire of Scripts, believing the fervor Nicholas and Marianna displayed would not be influenced, gave grudging consent to the union.

A month passed in a flurry of wedding preparations. Soon, friends came to witness the vows in a solemn ceremony at All Saints Episcopal Church on Dolores Street, and to dance their good wishes at the Mission Ranch reception. Marianna and Nicholas departed for Austria before the week was out.

This daughter of the Sire of Scripts basked in the allure of the diplomatic circuit. Her husband's attentions warmed her heart and kept her face aglow.

Marianna and Nicholas had three children in quick succession: two sons and a daughter. While Nicholas attended to diplomatic protocols, Marianna delighted her children with fascinating tales of intrigue and rescue.

In due time, Marianna found that diplomatic life wasn't as glamorous as it had at first appeared. Numerous parties served the same food, were attended by the same people, who were enthralled by the same prattle. Rumors abounded of Nicholas' not so clandestine trysts.

Years passed and Marianna rarely saw her sons, immersed as they were in their university studies. She looked on with sorrow and trepidation as a knight in shining armor whisked her dazzled daughter away.

A sense of despair gripped her soul; her children were grown; Nicholas disdained what was once the bliss of their marriage bed. She knew some comfort when her thoughts drifted back to the happier days in Carmel-by-the-Sea. She could hear the cadence of the Sire of Scripts and it momentarily lifted her spirits. One day in late fall, it frightened her to discover her mind's eye failed her. Her reverie didn't reveal the gnarled, mystic cypress trees shrouded in fog; missing was the feel of the wind blowing in her face. The sound of waves lapping toward her ankles eluded her. Even the white sand of Carmel was absent from her vision.

Shortly after her twenty-fifth wedding anniversary, she awoke to three words burning across her consciousness: "homesick," "lonely," and "unhappy." By every outward appearance, she had been leading a storybook life of diplomatic parties, concerts and plays. She received warm attention from outsiders, but little from Nicholas.

22

On a miserably cold winter's evening, word came of the death of her beloved Sire of Scripts. Marianna was plunged into grief, utterly bereft, a prisoner in the devil's own land of depression.

She spent most of her hours reading and studying. Slowly the power of words began to ease her spirit as she considered them along with the principles and truths she'd absorbed at the knee of her Sire of Scripts.

Late spring moved to early summer, and Marianna sat in the garden reflecting. She considered how to reverse unhappiness, isolation and homesickness. Marianna continued to read and reflect.

One day in the mail she received a large green book with a note written in elegant calligraphy: "Exercise your right to write your truth and share it. The rest, no doubt will unfold as it should." It was signed Corlis, Mistress of Agents and Publishers.

Marianna opened the book. She followed the exercises. She wrote and wrote, the words flowing from deep within. She filled the green book with the truths that she knew. Corlis, Mistress of Agents and Publishers, sold all her words to periodicals all over the land.

Now, if this were a typical fairytale, Nicholas would rue the lie he'd been living and try to make amends with phrases like, "Please forgive me, my dear Marianna," or "I've been such a cad, while you've been faithful and true. Forgive me, forgive me, please do," he'd have begged, contrition issuing from every pore.

However, in this fairytale, Nicholas held no further sway. "Fie on your old diplomacy! I'm going home to my lovely, literary principality of Carmel-by-the Sea." Marianna left Nicholas to fend for himself.

She lived happily ever after listening to the stories of a new crop of writers who came for tea in her lovely cottage by the sea.

THE ROAD
MARNIE SPERRY

The Road — a string of black asphalt
winding through mountains,
then, framed by golden wheat,
stretching as far as the eye can see,
    mile after mile
past lives of everyday folks just like us,
past hitchhikers trying to convey with a
    look and a thumb
why they are worthy of a ride,
past Mom and Pop diners,
Texaco gas stations,
and fast food drive-throughs.

The Road, a destination in and of itself,
a different story told by every car that passes.
Blazed by wagon wheels
    in years gone by,
now home to truckers feeding the country
with their delivered goods,
holding one place to another,
a lifeline to and through a nation,
binding it from coast to coast.

The Road, hypnotic on a clear dark night
as white lines loom,
then slip into blackness;

Mesmerizing on hot summer days
when eyelids grow heavy,
thoughts wander into dreams,
and blazing horns shock driver to wakefulness.

The Road, a literary treasure chest of signage,
huge signs selling America,
of license plates,
and bumper stickers,
and billboards
and graffiti by unknowns
who wish they were known.

The Road, final resting place
for empty beer bottles,
stale lunch leftovers,
yesterday's newspaper,
bits of this and that from here and there,
and a coyote that was too slow.

The Road, a lure for discontented souls,
an empty, unspoken notion
of better things down the line.
The Road holds promises for all,
a destination,
a means to an end,
a "get out of town quick",
but best of all,
"We're home!"

PACIFIC MIGRATION
LINDA GRANT

Oblivious to the storm breaking overhead
they frolic in pods of fours and threes
amid swollen waves and winter whitecaps.

Playing tag before arching their glistening backs
and disappearing.
Farther down the coast they emerge
sounding their return
a stream of mist spiraling upward.

It's late November
and like the Snow Goose
the Grey Whale travels south.

THE WINTER GUESTS

(Inspired by the short story, *Cat In The Rain*,
by Ernest Hemingway.)

KEN JONES

He put his pencil on the desk and closed the ledger. He could have let the books go a day or two, it being the off season, but the lessons his father had taught him were nestled too deep inside, more than simple habit. He could no more go to bed without tending to the day's ledger than he could be rude or indifferent to one of his guests. He dropped his glasses on the ledger and rubbed the deep grooves they'd pressed into the bridge of his nose. He switched off the light, closed his eyes and leaned back in his chair, listening to the rain dripping off the tile roof onto the gravel walkway outside his office window.

Over the steady rhythm of the rain, he heard her voice and thought again of the American girl in the room above him. When she'd come to the hotel three days earlier his first thought had been that she was a child. Tall and somewhat awkward, her fair skin and boyish look in stark contrast to the look of the man who had accompanied her. The man's weathered face and unruly manner suggested a stable hand more than a traveler. He remembered his surprise upon learning the two were husband and wife.

Something about the girl had charmed him. Perhaps it was the way she'd come to him timidly, almost apologetically, to tell him there were no towels in their room. A little thing, but she'd come with such politeness and deference that he'd immediately called for Maria and instructed the maid to supply towels to the young lady's room without delay. He had been moved by the girl's expression of appreciation for this simple act.

He heard the man's voice now from above, raised just enough to cause him to listen more intently though he could not make out the words. He heard the door to their room close and then her steps — they could be no one else's — on the stairs. She paused when she came to the doorway at the far end of his office. He stood and bowed in greeting. She was really quite beautiful, he thought. The light in the hallway fell across her face, accentuating its youth and innocence. She appeared more child-like as she stood framed by the doorway, twisting her hands at her slim waist.

"*Il piove*," she said, her voice a violin solo.

"*Si, si,*" he replied. "*Brutto tempo.* It's very bad weather."

She smiled and turned and continued toward the lobby. He sat heavily. Perhaps it was the rain, or the darkening sky, or the loveliness of the young girl...he felt his age tonight.

Maria hurried into the room and stood, head bowed, across the desk from him.

"What is it, Maria?" he asked.

"The woman is going out," the maid replied.

"She has no coat, she will be wet," he said absently, almost to himself.

"*Si, Padrone,*" the maid nodded.

"Quickly, take an umbrella and go with her," he said after a moment's thought. The maid raised her eyebrows in surprise, but only briefly.

"*Si, Padrone,*" she said and hurried toward the hall.

"And Maria!" he called, stopping the maid at the doorway. "Find out why she must go out on a night such as this."

"*Si, Padrone,*" the maid answered before disappearing down the hall.

Curious, he thought. He rose stiffly, stretching his arms and legs. Leaving the light off, he moved to the window and watched the two women, crouched beneath the umbrella, as

28

they walked past on the path. He could barely hear their voices. He heard Maria laugh, and then the two hurried past the window toward the lobby door. Very curious, he thought again. He sat at the desk and rubbed his aching knees. It's hard to be old, he thought, harder when it rains.

The girl came into his doorway again, shaking the water from her skirt. Droplets of rain glistened from her cropped hair in the hall light. Her eyes were big now and her mouth formed a small frown. She looked, to him, even younger than before. He nodded to her, not taking his eyes from hers, and her frown slowly became a smile. She seemed almost to bow before turning to run up the stairs.

He heard her door close above him as Maria came into the office, patting her hair and brushing the raindrops from her dress. Her expression was one of amusement and disbelief.

"Why did she go out?" he asked.

"*Il gatto*," the maid replied.

"*Il gatto?*"

"*Si, Padrone*. She saw a cat, probably the stray from the restaurant, under a table in the courtyard. She wanted the cat."

He smiled, then began to laugh softly to himself. "She wanted the cat."

"*Si, Padrone.*"

"Then, she shall have one," he said and watched the maid's expression of disbelief turn to one of astonishment. "Find Napoleon and take him to her room," he told the maid. "He's no doubt asleep on my bed."

"*Padrone?*" the maid questioned.

"Take her the cat," he said and turned his chair toward the window.

The sky outside his window now was the color of old pewter and the rain continued to fall. He heard Maria calling for Napoleon, who had apparently seen her coming. He heard the girl's voice in the room above, occasionally the man's. He poured a small glass from the bottle of Port in the bottom drawer of his desk and lit a cigarette. He watched the smoke rise against the darkening window.

After a few moments he heard Maria's footsteps on the stairs and then her knock at the girl's door. *"Avanti,"* he heard the man call. The door closed and the maid descended the stairs. As she passed his doorway, he could see the maid shaking her head and talking to herself.

Then from above he heard the girl's laughter. Light and free, it poured down and washed over him. He smiled and took a sip of Port, feeling its warming fingers move through him. He took another long draw on his cigarette, closed his eyes and rocked slowly in his chair as the sounds of the girl's laughter and the rain blended in the darkness around him.

EINSTEIN LIVES!

WALTER E. GOURLAY

December, 1999. End of the century, end of the millennium. The wind blew chill on my face as I hurried past the Central Park Zoo to my apartment on East 83rd, in my mittened hand the spatula I'd just bought in the Five and Ten.

"Excuse me, sir." A foreign accent. A panhandler? I stopped and faced him.

He shuffled over. I suddenly realized I'd seen that face a hundred times in news magazines and newsreels. Scraggly mustache, glasses, unruly gray hair and earmuffs. A pipe. "You know," I said, "you look like…"

"Albert Einstein," he interrupted. "I *am* Albert Einstein."

"Einstein is dead."

"Yes, I am. Or was. Or both. Or will be. Time is relative. Except for the speed of light, that is. I'm dead in one part of the space-time continuum, and alive in another. It's hard to explain."

"Well, Mr. Einstein…"

"Dr. Einstein, if you please."

I wondered what kind of squirrel food I'd come across. "Well, Dr. Einstein, what can I do for you?"

"I'd like to talk to you," he said. "First, I'll take us somewhere warmer." He took a slide rule out of his pocket. "I should be able to do this in my head," he apologized, "but I never was much good at math."

Suddenly, the zoo disappeared and we were standing in bright sunlight under a clear sky, on an ice shelf surrounded on three sides by water. In the distance, a group of birds resembling waiters were waddling into the water.

31

"Ah, pelicans," he said.

"Penguins," I corrected.

"Not pelicans?"

"Penguins."

"I can never remember which is which," he said.

"Dr. Einstein," I said. "This may be summer in the Antarctic but I'm freezing my balls off, and I'm going to need them tonight. Let's get out of here."

"Sorry," he said. "I misdirected us. When I was a clerk in Antwerp I was always misdirecting mail."

A crack appeared in the ice between us, and widened quickly. "Global warming," I told him. We began to float apart. I stretched out my hand, but he couldn't reach it. I extended the spatula. He gripped it and pulled me toward him. I scrambled onto his slab of ice. Under our weight, it began to crack. He took out his slide rule and calculated.

Abruptly, we were in Key West, under a warm, semitropical sun. Large winged brown birds, looking like pterodactyls, flapped overhead.

"Pelicans?" he asked.

"Pelicans."

"Ah." He nodded.

"Nice," I said. "But could you get me home to New York, please? I'm expecting a lady friend for dinner." He reached for his slide rule again.

We were suddenly in Wan Chai in Hong Kong. Then the *funicolare* on Capri. He was getting faster, but not more accurate. Grand Canyon. Penguins. "Stop!" I yelled. I recognized the Central Park Zoo.

It was still freezing. I clutched my trusty spatula. Never leave home without it.

In my third-floor walkup, I offered him my best Scotch. He gulped it down enthusiastically, wetting his mustache in the process. I was getting fond of the old codger.

For the next hour or so, he quizzed me about life and the technology at the end of the Twentieth Century. My computer and the Internet fascinated him. "Amazing, amazing," he said. I explained our fears about the so-called Y2K bug. "They're expecting all our computers to crash," I said, "because the programmers didn't account for the end of the century."

"How could they be so stupid?" he asked, shaking his head. We turned on my TV. After a few minutes of commercials and the ubiquitous juvenile sitcoms he turned it off and shook his head. "Such a waste of technology," he said. Then he told me what was really bothering him. "I'll never forgive myself for convincing President Roosevelt to make the atom bomb. It was a horrible mistake. The Japanese were already defeated. No need to drop that horrible thing. I want to change Roosevelt's mind."

"Can you alter history?" I asked.

"I can try," he said, and extended his hand. "Thank you for everything. Have a happy New Year." He took out his slide rule and disappeared.

That night Gina, my current girlfriend, came over and I cooked dinner. As we watched the snow flickering past the window, I told her about my day. She laughed in that lovely throaty voice she had.

"Boy," she said, "what an imagination. Einstein, yet. How many years has he been dead?"

"Einstein lives," I said.

"Like Elvis," she said, pulling me into the bedroom. "Come on, darling, let's us live a little."

A couple of days after New Year's, I phoned her. "What about the Y2K bug?" I asked.

"What's a Y2K bug?"

"That's the point. There wasn't any and nobody can figure out why not."

"So?"

"Einstein lives," I said.

"So what about the Adam bomb?"

"Adam bomb?"

"You said he was going to stop the Adam bomb."

"What the hell's an Adam bomb? I never heard of it."

"You said."

"Must be something I read in a science fiction story. Are you coming over tonight?"

"With or without my toothbrush?"

"Don't leave home without it."

A low chuckle in response.

A few days later, the *New York Herald* reported that the ozone hole had begun to disappear now that cars were using solar power and fuel cells.

That night I went out to look at the moon, where we'd put up the space station during the McGovern administration in the seventies. I watched the Mars transport coming in.

Einstein lives, I thought. Huh? What the hell did Einstein have to do with anything? He's been dead for ages. Then Gina came over and we turned my attention to loftier matters.

THE WRITER

CAROL BROWN KAUFFMANN

I am a creator and architect
of words.
I give warmth to the sun,
coolness to the moon,
fragrance to the flowers,
flesh to the living.

Without me, the universe
has no meaning.
It is a silent abyss.
As I write,
birds begin to sing,
oceans roar,
clouds swirl.

As I describe,
cats begin to purr,
horses gallop,
humans love.

When I am angry,
there are world wars.
When I am sad,
there are floods.
When I am hungry,
there is famine.

This is the power of words!

THE STRAWBERRY ROAN
Harold E. Grice

Oh! The Strawberry Roan
Oh! That Strawberry Roan
Sixteen hands tall at the wither
Could pull the buckboard, the plow
    or the flivver
His Roman nose made him stubborn
    and dumb
But once gotten started
Oh! How he would run
So tall was the roan, that his back to gain
I had to shimmy the leg,
    grab a handful of mane
But once aboard, it was "HI HO SILVER!!"
He was my horse, I'll love him forever

Oh! And how could he run
And Oh! How this tad had fun
No matter it was that he was left over
And we became the ones of a kind
That we naturally came together
It seemed we understood each other
    Oh! My Strawberry Roan
    Oh! My Strawberry Roan
I hope you're there in grasses of heaven
Where you don't have to be so gol-dang
    stubborn
And we'll ride again when I get there

Goodbye! My Strawberry Roan
    Goodbye! My Strawberry Roan
        Goodbye! My Strawberry Roan.
      Goodbye.

The reason I wrote this poem is that I left the ranch and the strawberry roan, never to return. Never again would I ride him. And I never knew his end. I can't imagine it was good.

We moved to the ranch after Mother married William (Bill) Brown (a grass widower). We found ourselves on a ranch of some two thousand acres or so.

Our new home was the old ranch house. It consisted of nine rooms and a bath. The kitchen had a butane gas stove and refrigerator. The kitchen and the rest of the house were heated by stoves, the wood kitchen range and the pot-bellied living room wood burner. We learned to cut the wood for the wood stoves.

The old house had patented wood siding and a plaster interior. The floor plan was 1920's country. The front door entered on a long hallway that ran through the house to end in the bathroom at the back wall. The bathroom did not have an inside toilet when we moved in. Mom soon had this corrected. Along the south was a series of four bedrooms, all nearly the same size with the exception of the one just opposite the kitchen, which was maybe a third larger. This was Mom and Brown's room. To the north side of the hall was first the parlor/living room, then the dining room, then the kitchen with a pantry and back porch dividing the remainder of that side.

The first bedroom was taken over by my sister; the second was Jerry Brown's, Bill Brown's daughter by his previous marriage. She was the girl side of twins. Her twin brother had been trampled to death by horses in a corral. This apparently led to the divorce.

The farthest back room was for us three boys.

To the parlor was assigned the old Oriental rug, the nice old horsehide couch and chair, and the piano. The piano was always a mystery. A friend from Los Angeles could play anything "by ear." Sister Jean could play things with practice. I understood the principles of this thing but could never solve the function. My mind always chided me because I would never give to the practice the same effort I gave to the thought of practice.

37

When we arrived at the ranch, there were just three horses: Bill Brown's small sorrel quarter horse, Gene Rhode's buckskin (Bucky), and an old plug of a workhorse. It was decided by Mom and Brown to find some more horseflesh.

(I spent a good deal of time worrying about what to call my stepfather. I knew he and Mother were husband and wife, which is like mother and father, but I still could not push aside my own father. To say father, dad, or pa is to give that person that identity. I had tried it a couple times but it just didn't set comfortable on me. I kept searching for a name I could use.

I ultimately resolved this by not using any name at all when I addressed him. I found it more comfortable to just start talking. It was easier to address him without a name being offered than it was to use a name for this man, a habit that has followed me through my years. And as an apology to my mother and as a resolution of the idea, he was probably an all-right person and I got to like him some, but then I have always been accused of accepting everyone no matter the pedigree. But even so he was not my father, dad or pa.)

It was not long before they found and purchased, probably with Mother's money, four additional horses.

The introduction of more horses to the ranch required a readjustment of the pecking order. Before, there was Gene Rhode's Bucky, my stepfather's quarter horse, and the old plug. These horses actually belonged to someone. The new ones sorta didn't belong to anyone in particular. The problem was that there were now four horses and five riders.

'Bucky' and Bill Brown's horses were never included in this count. This meant there were never enough horses. Someone would have to go in the car, or truck, or walk. I was often the one who got to take the easy way and go in the car. But it was considered a kindness because I was such a puny kid, susceptible to colds and etcetera, etcetera. Besides, "He could never keep up."

Also, I was the youngest. As the youngest in a large family, one has few choices but many opportunities.

But it so happened that the four new horses consisted of

a chubby little part quarter horse named Man"; a tall and gangly roper named "High" with the unique soft stepping "single-foot gait"; a medium Guerra broomtail that was a horse and a half (at show-off someone called him "Cricket" and it stuck); and a tall, Roman-nosed, sharp bodied, long legged, dumb, stubborn strawberry roan.

He became known as "The Roan," "The Strawberry Roan," "That Horse," "That God-Damned Horse," "That Son-of-a-Bitch Horse," "I'm gonna shoot that Son-of-a-Bitch Horse" and "That Hard-Headed God-Damned Roman-Nosed Stupid No-Good Son-of-a-Bitch Roan."

No one really liked the Strawberry Roan. No one really wanted to have him and consider him their own. I kind of identified with that and we took to each other. I got him by default. He was the last one left after the mounts of preference had been roped out of the corral, because this horse couldn't do anything useful very long without being contrary.

"Man" could start a steer then quarter the hind legs so's you could lay the rope and let the steer run into it. "High" could run you to the head and hold stride with the fastest outlaw, and his motion was so smooth you could go to sleep. "Cricket" was so "gad-damn" quick she could turn on a dime and give a nickel's change.

The Strawberry Roan was slow to start, impossible to stop and might turn in a country mile. But then again, might not. To swing a loop from his back was a chancy thing. If you touched an ear, that old Roan would stand on end. If you did drop the loop on a steer, the Roan might stop and then again he might not. One wise old cow that had been roped several times had learned to stop when the loop dropped on her neck. Well, I dropped the rope on her and jerked the slack out. I whoa'd the Roan. He was disinclined to stop. Ran right into the poor old cow. Knocked her bottom over milk jug.

At times, to ask this horse to obey the rein was to invite a frightening rear. Straight up on his hind legs he'd go.

But then at day's end when the fancy horses were spent and the prancers were foot weary, the Strawberry Roan was

39

still just the "Strawberry Roan." No different, no more tired than I.

And even then when we'd pull into a new situation his head'd come up and he'd pay attention. You just knew he would do something exciting. Unusual, stupid or contrary, but exciting.

I started riding him by default and ended up riding him by preference. I used that horse at every chance. This doesn't mean he became a good horse, or a smart horse, or even maybe a passable horse. He never did. He just happened to be the horse I used. We got along because I learned to anticipate his contrary ways. I found ways to get done what I wanted without too much trouble. And maybe he got to know that when I lost concentration it was time to bring back reality by rearing, running away, or ducking under a low, low limb. Very often it seemed it was just something to show just how dumb I was and how stubborn he was. At any rate it was a passably good relationship. I hope he is now wherever I will go, whenever.

One time we were coming down off the hill, pushing a few cows that needed a boost. I let the old Roan have the rein because despite it all, he was sometimes a decent cow horse. He shoved those cows out to the trail. Then he decided that with all that open ground he ought to just stretch out. I'd had the idea we should haze those cows into the lane.

Well, the Roan took the bit in his mouth and away we went. This old Roan could clamp down on a bit, Spanish or modified, and you just couldn't get a response. He was surely a hard-mouthed horse. Sometimes it was suggested his mouth was made of iron. When he took a notion, he wouldn't answer to the rein. Off the hill. Through the squirrel field (had he stepped in a hole it would have broken his leg and I would have been catapulted into oblivion. He never stepped in a hole. Things like this always made me wonder just how dumb this horse was.) Out across the meadow to the trail that followed the gully. I figured I would turn him across the gully at the turn. This gully was about eight feet deep and ten feet across.

40

He would have to stop. I could get him under control. We got to the turn; I sawed the reins across his neck with the right rein separate in my hand, pulling his head around; I had him headed for the gully; his eyes were wide open, all bugged out, looking at everything. He's gotta stop.

He didn't. He jumped the gully. I was set back in the saddle, all set for him to stop, so my weight was all wrong. When he jumped I got off balance. Out of the saddle, rolled up over the cantle. My toes were pointed to heaven. I was well on my way to losing it all. Fortunately, I was still in the stirrups. I grabbed any leather I could reach and hung on. I finally got straightened up with only a crick in my back, a Yankee blush, and a ten-dollar mad. I swear that stupid horse was laughing. He slowed to a lope and he stopped. Then, while I was checking out all those parts of me stressed beyond belief in the jump, he headed back and shushed all the cows down off the hill and into the lane. Maybe it was just that his life wasn't exciting enough.

One time, my sister Jean was riding him. They stopped to water in the creek. She didn't want him to drink too much and founder. Cricket had died earlier that year from heart seizure after a hard day, so she kept trying to get his head up and away from the water. He didn't appreciate that kind of interference. He reared so quickly and so high, Jean tumbled out of the saddle into the water. She was really pretty upset at that God-Damned Roan.

I never worried about that sort of thing. If the stupid horse wanted to drink the creek dry and founder, that was his affair. Mostly he just gurgled after tanking up. The thing he liked to do on hot days was get to the horse trough, shove his head down into the water all the way up to his eyes, then pull it out and shake water and snot all over. Anyone not aware of this got a surprise shower.

That Roan would get to rearing with me. The incidents of rearing would increase to a point where riding was pretty much a lot of ups and downs. When I really got exasperated I would do several things. One was to get a large rotten limb and as he would start to rear, I would clobber him over the head. It got his attention with the smash on the noggin and all that bark and rotten wood falling all over. He would be pretty good for a while.

The very ultimate, if it became really unbearable, was when he reared to his highest, I would hold on to the off rein and slide out over his back and pull him over. That old horse would go down real hard, grunt and flail the air with his hooves. He'd scramble to his feet round-eyed and seemingly embarrassed.

After the initial exhilaration of triumph, I always felt kind of mean. But he wouldn't rear for a long time.

On the other side of the coin, I could catch him in the field, shimmy up a leg and get on and ride him into the barn and corrals with nothing more than leaning and leg pressure. Or on a lazy day, I could lie on his back in the shade under the trees and just watch the red-headed woodpeckers stuffing acorns in new holes in the old oak, follow the swallows arching the sky uppity times, gritting mud for mud houses up under the eaves, or just lie there on his back in the horse smell and warm air.

During the summer, everyone was off harvesting. Brown harvested grain as a business. This required several helpers. At eleven going on twelve, I was still too young to harvest. The other kids were older and they fit the bill fine.

Jean drove the tractor, Roy sewed the sacks and John jigged, that is, he put the sacks under the grain spouts and lifted them to Roy. This left no one at the farm except me to milk the cows, slop the hogs and throw hay down to the cows. So that's what I did. Other than that and shocking hay or hoeing weeds once in a while, my time was pretty much free. So I had time for interesting things.

Jerry and I got the Roan to pull with a harness. I made a sled out of an old kid's wagon body and cut runners and bolted cross members. Brown thought it was okay though he didn't like me using up his nails and bolts, but Jerry was involved and that made it okay. We had the Roan pull us around in the yard. Brown even suggested that I put metal runners on it.

There was all sorts of abandoned equipment about the ranch so I had no trouble finding two strips of metal a couple of inches wide and long enough to armor the runners. With these on the runners, the sled slid along great.

Jerry and I had great fun going about, one of us on the Roan and the other in the sled. It really seemed fast, being that close to the ground when the horse was running. And every once and a while a large dirt clod would come whizzing by.

One field was kind of marshy. It grew a great stand of thistles, the ones with the big spiky heads. We would get the Roan to race around in a circle and just mow those thistles down. 'Cept once. Jerry was on the Roan and I was in the sled. Suddenly things weren't going so well. The Roan started kicking and jumping like crazy and Jerry either got bucked off or jumped off. That horse got to whizzing along. Being so close to the ground, the speed seemed much too fast to bail out, so I just hung on.

Finally the Roan came to a stop by the fence, rubbing his tail across his rump. I discovered one of the thistle heads had gotten up under the after harness strap. He was getting stuck something fierce. He was all right after that but I had to lead him back with Jerry in the sled because she was overly cautious.

One time we were just loafing along the lane coming back down from the hill. I was riding and Jerry was in the sled. The Roan lifted his tail and let out a long gas. Then I heard the plop, plop, plop of horse apples hitting the ground. The sled slide noise had changed. I turned around to look and there was Jerry standing about a hundred feet back. I turned the Roan around and went back.

"What's the matter?"

Jerry was indignant. "I am not riding in there with your horse doing that."

"Well, he's through."

"I'm not riding in there no more."

"O.K." So we switched and Jerry rode the horse. Interesting how little things can change stuff.

Later on we broke Bucky to the harness too. Now we had a team. Funny looking team though. The Roan was about a foot taller than Bucky. But they would pull all right. The Roan wouldn't out-pull Bucky because along with everything else, he was lazy. We hitched the Roan and Bucky to the buckboard. It was great fun to visit up and down the valley in the buckboard. In a buckboard you can ride along nonchalant-like, hearing the meadowlarks, the quail and the whistle of doves winging overhead. You can smell the grass and greasewood cooking in the sun. You can just lie back and enjoy life. Once you turn around the horses will take you home. They always know the way home.

But that became boring.

So we took them into the hayfield. The hay had been cut and taken in, so the field had only short stalks remaining. We got the horses going and making sharp turns. The wheels kicked up dirt and chaff. It was great fun. We even got the buckboard to raise up on two wheels a time or two.

Then just to see how fast we could go, we lined them out across the field. Of course the Roan ran away.

Boy! We were going fast!

We hauled on the reins. Bucky tried to stop but the Roan was so large and powerful that Bucky just got dragged along. He had to run or get dragged. He ran.

The end of the field was coming up and Jerry gave me the reins. She was wide-eyed and hanging on.

I tried to turn that Roan, but he had the bit in his teeth and wouldn't listen.

The field ended in a shallow rise and then a grass-covered hill. It didn't look bad so I figured to let them tire pulling up the hill. That Roan didn't like to work too hard. He'd stop.

We approached the hill and Jerry was on the side of the brake so I had to lean over to get my foot on it, and I was pushing with all my might and sawing on the reins. The Roan was fighting the bit and throwing his head up and down. I had to ease off. I was afraid he wouldn't see where he was going and fall. Then we would go over the top and be in a real mess.

44

We hadn't realized that the reason the hill wasn't farmed was because it was a big pile of rocks.

As we went up the slope, the buckboard bounced and lurched. Jerry slid off the seat, starting over the edge under the wheels. I quick got an arm around her but it wasn't really enough. She was still slipping. The horses were still going and the buckboard was bouncing violently.

I managed to get a bite of her shirt with my teeth; this let me hold her steady. Gathering all my strength, I held her back with my teeth, lurched my arm around her, got a better hold and hauled her back onto the seat. Onto my lap, actually. I held on to her with all my strength. I pushed that brake pedal until I felt it bend.

The Roan was getting tired and coming to his senses. The horses slowed and came to a stop just as the buckboard dropped over a large rock.

Poor little Bucky stood spraddle-legged and winded. The Roan took a few good huffs and let out a long sigh. Then he looked around with his big eyes as if to ask if we'd had a good ride.

Jerry and I got down from the buckboard and just stood there looking at each other. I asked if she was okay and she just nodded her head "yes."

I didn't think to beat up on the Roan. I was concerned about getting the buckboard off the hill without tearing it up. I managed to coax the horses to turn the buckboard so I could work it back down to the field.

We walked back to the ranch, probably a mile, leading the horses and buckboard. Jerry was very quiet. After a while I became quiet too. At the ranch, I put the buckboard away, unharnessed the horses and turned them out. I went down and got the cows in and started my chores.

That evening at dinner, Brown and my brothers and sister were back from harvesting and we were all busy eating when Jerry started talking about the runaway. I was really chagrined. I usually got in trouble for anything that went wrong regardless of whose idea it was. For my part I would have just as soon it hadn't been mentioned. But there it was. Jerry telling about the runaway and the bouncing buckboard and almost getting thrown out. Brown was scowling deeper and darker all the time. I knew it was not going to be good for me, it never was.

Finally when Jerry finished, Brown looked at me and stated, "I haven't had to whip you in a long time but I guess that was just an oversight. Go find a switch."

My fate was sealed.

Jerry was standing next to her father and shook his arm. She was looking right at me. "Daddy," she said, "Harold saved my life."

Brown visibly diminished. He just became less sure, less hostile.

He said, "Well, okay then. Don't do it again."

And we never did.

A BRIEF INTERRUPTION
MARTIN DODD

The last man on earth sat in his study, reading by the last light of day. There was a knock on the door. He flinched, taking a sudden breath, and looked up. His mouth opened then closed. Slowly, he exhaled. His eyes wandered to the books that lined the walls, then back to the door. He blinked and swallowed, then resumed reading.

CHOICE
MARTIN DODD

Memory, perception, expectation.
Reality?
No.
All imagined.
So choose.

HURRICANE SEASON
ILLIA THOMPSON

Inside the small house on Avenue S and ½
in Galveston, Texas
I run myself around
from room to room
in many circles
and when I cannot catch my breath
I sink into a puddle
and melt into blackness.

I awaken certain that I am in heaven
as flowers send sweetness to me:
roses, sticky pasty hollyhocks
and lilies that smell old before they fade.
I am too young for heaven at ten years old
and find that I am in a hospital
whiteness around my room
Nurses, Doctors, and I am told
a white powder, "Sulfa,"
saved my life.

I collect nickels in a piggy bank.
Each clink tells me I let them
give me another shot and
the prick of the needle hurts less
when followed by the sound that can become
a whole ice cream cone when I go home.
I rest and sleep and feel a bit like MADELINE,
I get visits from Mother and Daddy and my
    sister, Eva.
She's probably glad to have our parents alone.
Does she miss me?

Food begins to taste again.
Red Jell-O melts into juice
if I let it stay in my mouth long enough.
Orange Popsicles do too
I get cream of wheat
like they sing about on
"Let's Pretend."
And I do pretend to be
Sleeping Beauty, The Ugly Duckling,
Snow White,
and even maybe that
I'll never get well and be myself
before I melted.

"Pneumonia," Mother tells me,
"You almost died" and
I remember stories about
how tiny I was when I was born
and that then, too, I "almost died."

And I think of all the
Jewish children in the war that I know about
though no one really told me,
about how they have no
"almost" before "died."

I look at my arm.
No scars from the shots
that will make me rich
but I am more than
just a little girl getting well.

I write inside my head:
"Why do I live while others die?"

49

DISCONNECTED

KEN JONES

Jerry Miller sat on his usual barstool, holding his usual brew, telling the usual lies to the other regulars at the Tip-In Bar near the corner of Vermont and Grant. He'd just regained his composure after losing it completely over a joke one his friends had told when the bartender carried a black rotary phone over and put it down on the bar in front of him.

"Your sister-in-law's looking for you again, Jer," he said.

Jerry checked his watch, eight thirty. *Way too early for anybody to be looking for me,* he thought. He rolled his eyes for the benefit of the others, who had slipped back into uncontrolled laughter. "What's the matter now?" he barked into the phone.

"It's...your brother, Jerry...he's been shot!" Jerry's sister-in-law said through wrenching sobs. Jerry heard the baby crying in the background.

"*What*?" he yelled, holding his free hand over his ear. "What did you say?"

"It's Tom!" she screamed back, "He's been shot! They just took him. Oh God, Jerry...I think he's gonna die!"

"Who took him? Where?" Jerry asked, frantically trying to shake the beer out of his thoughts. His friends at the bar were quiet now.

"The paramedics. I think they said they were going to Bayview. Oh, God Jerry, what am I gonna do?"

"Just stay with the kids!" Jerry said. "I'll call you from the hospital."

Jerry hung up, drained his beer, and ran for the door.

He didn't hear the protests of some of his clearer thinking buddies who called to him to calm down a little before he took off.

He ran to his new silver Navigator, climbed in and burned rubber out of the parking lot, nearly clipping a black Jaguar that had just turned the corner off Vermont. Jerry could see that the man driving was on a cell phone. *Asshole*, Jerry thought, *could'a killed me.*

Jerry made the turn up Grant, following the Jaguar. The more he thought about it, the more pissed off he became. "I'll show that son of a bitch," Jerry said aloud, and started flashing his high beams. He ran up on the black car, only meaning to threaten the driver, but he misjudged his speed and tapped the rear bumper, causing the car ahead to swerve. *Shit*, thought Jerry, and dropped back. Then he saw the driver raise his hand.

"Son of a bitch flipped me off," Jerry said. He accelerated again, intending to ram the car this time, but he misjudged the approach and fell short.

The Jaguar took the freeway onramp and Jerry followed. He charged again and this time made solid contact. The Jag spun to the top of the curve.

As Jerry merged onto the freeway, he looked back to see the Jag's headlights wheel wildly across the ramp then disappear over the edge. *Serves the bastard right*, Jerry thought. *Hang up and drive, man.*

He arrived at Bayview Hospital a few minutes later. As he ran into the emergency room waiting area, a woman wearing soiled green scrubs stopped him. The stitched nametag over her pocket read "Bradley."

"Where is he?" Jerry demanded.

"Calm down," the woman said. "Who are you here to see?"

Jerry took a deep breath and answered her.

"Your brother is in extremely serious condition, sir," the woman explained. "He's in the operating room. We're waiting for the surgeon. He's the best chest man in the area and he *should* already be here. We're trying to confirm his arrival time now."

* * *

"Oh, no," Dr. William Adams sighed, reaching for his buzzing pager. "Not tonight!"

"That's not the hospital is it, Bill?" his wife asked, pushing her dinner plate away and slowly folding her napkin.

"'Fraid so, hon," the doctor said. "I hate this, but I've got to go, it's a stat code. Finish your dinner, honey. I'll get back as soon as I can."

"I'll finish my wine and get a cab. I'll see you at home later. I hate this too, dear, but you must really be needed or they wouldn't have paged you. Not tonight. You go on. I'll be fine."

The valet held open the driver's side door and the doctor slid behind the wheel. As he pulled onto the street, he lifted his cell phone from its holder on the dash and keyed the speed dial number for the hospital. His call was answered on the second ring.

"Bayview," a voice said.

"This is Adams, what's up?"

"We have a gunshot, chest, male, twenty-ish. Being prepped now. Didn't want to bother you on your anniversary, doctor, but the ER staff is swamped with a bus rollover and, well, the gunshot can't wait and there's just nobody else."

"Who's handling the prep?" he asked, making the turn on Grant with one hand, narrowly missing a silver SUV pulling out of a parking lot near the corner.

"Dr. Bradley," said the voice in his cell phone.

"Patch me through, can you...*Jesus*! What's that guy doing?" A silver SUV, with high beams flashing, had tapped his rear bumper causing his car to fishtail.

Adams could see the driver in his mirrors, he looked angry. "*Damn it!*" he whispered. "What's the matter with that jerk? Where are the cops when you need them?" There was no time to bother with it now; he waved off the bump and kept driving.

He held the cell phone with his hunched shoulder now, using both hands to thread his way through the traffic. He saw the freeway on-ramp up ahead; the hospital was only minutes away.

"Bradley here," a woman's tired voice said.

"What've we got?" Adams asked.

"Male, about twenty-five, two bullets through the left lung, we suspect a nicked aorta. Stable now, but you'd better hurry."

"Okay, I should be there in less than five minutes. Where do you have him?" In his mirror he could see the SUV behind him, rushing and pulling back.

"OR four," Bradley answered.

"Okay, thanks. See you soon." He ended the call and tossed the phone down on the passenger seat.

The flashing headlights followed him as he started up the onramp. They dropped back and then charged again.

The SUV hit the right rear of Adams' car hard. Adams fought for control as the car spun into the turn. Only then did he realize he hadn't fastened his seat belt. The car left the ramp and tumbled down the embankment, throwing him from the driver's seat and crushing him under the rolling vehicle.

Over the sounds of hisses, hot metal ticking and the gradually slowing intermittent scrape of rubber against twisted sheet metal, the ringing of a cell phone rose from the wreckage.

LAUNDRY

WALTER E. GOURLAY

There were six of us in the jeep, bouncing along the noisy, dirty back alley that served as a street in this part of Naples. We slowed down as we came to the University that was our bivouac, honking our horn to let the sentinel know there was a war going on, and he should open the heavy iron gate to let us through. That was when we noticed this girl.

She was standing on the other side of the alley, away from the University, her back pressed against the dingy, crumbling wall that had been stained and worn with the offal of centuries. She wasn't doing anything, just standing there as though she had nothing better to do. That wasn't so strange when you knew our camp; there were always girls hanging around, and it wasn't because they were waiting for Christmas, either.

"There's some new talent," said Karsky.

She didn't look up and meet our eyes the way the other girls do, but kept her eyes on the ground, apparently studying the manure left there by the last donkey cart. She had a pale thin face without makeup that looked as though it had just been scrubbed; her white cotton dress was remarkably clean and had been carefully pressed.

"She looks like somebody's kid sister waiting after school," I said. Judging from what you could see of her legs, which were bare from her knees to her sandals, and from what was under the light blue sweater she wore over her dress, she couldn't have been more than fifteen.

Karsky laughed. "The only classes they have in there now are done 'by the numbers.' I'll teach her what she wants to know."

54

"Hell," said one of the others. "You couldn't teach her anything she doesn't know already." He leaned out of the jeep. "Hey, Baby!" he called. She didn't look up.

"Leave her alone," I said. "She looks like a nice kid."

"Then what's she doing around here?" asked Karsky.

I had no answer to that.

The doors miraculously opened and we passed inside, into the courtyard built five centuries before, lined with ancient and venerable marble statues of some very ancient and venerable gentlemen who looked and wondered at the daily doings of our very rational Army. Right now the courtyard was a mess hall because it was noon, so I sat down and forgot everything else, as was my custom while I had what they called chow under the chipped nose of a very reactionary-looking old gent whose name, I think, was Luigi Something-Or-Other. He looked pained at the idea of soldiers eating warmed over "C" Rations.

"Brother, you don't know the half of it," I told him. Then I washed my greasy kit in the cistern that dated from the Fourteenth Century, and which, they said, had no bottom, judging from the things that were known to have been thrown in there since. That would make quite a book if anybody cared to write it.

I washed my face in the place called "Professors Only," and got my pass, an illegibly mimeographed piece of paper that would entitle me to go down to the Red Cross and spend the rest of the afternoon there in utter boredom.

As I stepped away from the massive iron gate I noticed the girl again, and was ready to pass by with no more than the usual, polite glance at her legs, when she spoke.

"*Signor*," she said. Now I'll have you know that was a pretty good line for an opener. I'd been called "Joe" before, and most of the other names that were more usual and less printable, but I'd never before been honored with the title of "*Signor*." It was equivalent to nobility in this part of Naples, and I wasn't aware that my escutcheon was showing.

"*Si, signorina?*" I inquired politely. I decided she must be very young and inexperienced.

"Do you have any laundry, *Signor?*"

I hadn't expected to discuss laundry after such an exalted beginning. Her Italian was still very correct and formal, so I decided that with her the subject of dirty wash was one to be approached with due respect and reverence. I shook my head in what I hoped was a reverent manner, and wondered why she was trying to find a customer here, where the laundry business had been painlessly monopolized for some time back by the one or two families who also handled our black market trade with a minimum of effort and a maximum of altruism, if you were to believe them.

"No," I said, "I already have a family that does my laundry." I didn't say what else they did, which covered the seven mortal sins and a few more besides. It wasn't a fit subject for the tender ears of a young girl who addressed me as "*Signor.*"

"But they are dirty," she said, "and they probably steal from you." She was sure to be right about that, and she knew it. She went on, looking into my eyes and speaking very gravely. "They do all the soldiers' clothes in one pot, to save soap so they can sell it on the black market. When you get your laundry back it's just as dirty as when you sent it. We wash your clothes separately. And besides," she said, adding the clincher, "I bring your laundry to you when it's done, and don't ask you to come and get it."

She had a good point there. Besides, she looked pretty, she looked nice, and she looked clean, and I liked the way her black hair was neatly tied behind her with a little red ribbon, and I liked the way she spoke Italian, clearly and musically, not like the *wallios* of the alleys. Besides, I felt sorry for her.

"I'll get you some laundry," I said.

I went inside, into the room which had once been a classroom devoted to higher learning, now tastefully furnished with twenty cots, each depressingly alike, with a GI blanket folded double according to regulations on each, and a gas mask hanging aesthetically from the foot. I dumped my barracks bag on the floor and counted out quickly the various dirty

56

handkerchiefs, towels, socks, shorts and undershirts that were the accumulation of a week's goldbricking. I threw a pair of wine-soaked trousers on top and tied it all into a slightly soiled suntan shirt, knotting the arms together tightly. I pulled a cake of dirty laundry soap from the towel to which it had become stuck, and inserted it into the bundle, then picked it all up and carried it out to her.

"Did you write your name on it?" she asked.

"No," I said. "You do it when you get home. The name is Tino."

"Tin-o," she repeated, tasting it. "Did you include the soap?"

"*Si.*"

She reached for the bundle in her hand, then hesitated. "Don't you want to come to see where I live?" she asked. "Then you will be able to find us in case you need your laundry in a hurry."

I recognized the wisdom of what she said. It was always better to be able to locate your laundry in case you had to move out. In Naples it was always better to locate your laundry anyway.

"Is it far?" I asked.

"Five minutes," she said. I shouldn't have asked. That was the standard time unit in Naples, and meant anything from fifteen minutes to an hour.

"O.K.," I said, figuring the Red Cross wouldn't change much while I was gone. She reached for the bundle. "I'll carry it," I told her.

"I'll take it," she said, pulling.

"I'll take it, *Signorina*. It's much too heavy for you on such a hot day." I swung it under my arm. She led the way down the alley, her short legs moving quickly to match my stride. She had nice legs.

We walked past the hovels that had been built in the Middle Ages, where families still lived, slept, and died in the same medieval squalor. Old men were boiling chestnuts in iron pots; they looked up as we passed, uncomprehendingly, then looked down again without expression. Two children, a boy and a girl, naked except for filth, were combing the alley for cigarette butts dropped by the Americans. Shutters opened slightly as we passed, and faces stared out, looking without hope for some evil with which to brighten the hopeless monotony of existence. See Naples and die, I thought, remembering the tourists' proverb.

"The *bassifondi*," she said. I'd heard the phrase before. It meant the "lower depths," and described accurately the stinking, suffering mass of humanity that made up the bulk of the city's population, packed full and starving in the back alleys where tourists never went.

We passed a dirty, crumbling building; it had a big sign saying "Off Limits To American Troops." Two GI's were coming out of the entrance, blinking in the strong sunlight. Then they saw us and walked quickly away, their hands in their pockets. They turned the first corner into another alley, out of our sight.

"Two girls live up there," she said. "They got tired of eating chestnuts."

I looked at her. "Don't you think it's better to eat chestnuts than to lose your self-respect?"

She looked at the ground. "You've never lived on chestnuts," she said. "There is no self-respect when one is very poor. Those girls lost nothing. Self-respect is only for the rich and for the Americans to hold up to them so they can think they are superior."

I kept quiet after that.

Soon we emerged into the modern world, on Corso Umberto, the busy bustling thoroughfare that runs from Via Roma to Piazza Garibaldi, where trolleys clang loudly and pedestrians scamper; where, in this Year of Our Lord 1944, G.I.'s from twenty-seven nations swaggered or staggered past exotic displays of silks and worsteds, precious gems and chocolates, fine liquors and ultra-smart radios fresh from the factories: Corso Umberto, where, they said, anything could be had for a price, from a cabinet minister to a GI truck, or the honor of your neighbor's sister.

We dodged a jeep that must have had it in for Americans, and crossed the Corso. We turned down toward the port, through the section where the working people had lived, now a mountainous heap of rubble left there by American bombers as a gesture of solidarity with the Italian people oppressed by Fascists, as the radio said. We stopped in front of a building that the bombers had only half missed.

"I live here," she said, "on the third floor."

The ground floor was a jumble of masonry, broken pipes, wooden beams and fallen plaster. "How do you get up there?" I asked.

"I'll show you." She led me through a path in the rubble, a path that led to a dark, evil-smelling hole that had been the entrance to an air-raid shelter. We went down a short ladder that was invisible in the darkness. The air was damp. In the shelter at the bottom she found a candle and lit it. The flame gleamed strangely on the walls and the low ceiling, reminding me of some early Christian crypt. Her face, too, was softly and brightly illuminated, like the statue of a Madonna. There were benches, half-visible in the gloom. She stood quietly for a moment.

"We are well protected from thieves here, you see. They could never find the way in the dark. It is very dark down here without a candle." She looked at the one in her hand for a moment. "Follow me," she said.

We went up a narrow wooden staircase at the other end of the shelves to the second floor, where she blew out the candle and put it on a shattered bookcase. There was a litter of broken furniture, scattered books, and plaster dust, the specks of which danced slowly in the sunlight.

"The people who lived here died in the bombardment," she said. We climbed an iron stairway to the third floor, where we were blocked by a heavy wooden door.

"My home," she said, and knocked. "Mamma!"

"Lydia?" The voice came from within.

"*Si*, Mamma." The door opened. I saw a small, tired-looking old lady, cleanly dressed in a black dress that bore signs of constant and careful mending. She smelled of soap.

"Mamma, this is Tino," said Lydia. "He has given me some laundry. And he speaks Italian, Mamma!"

The old lady smiled stiffly. "Come in. It is not often one finds an American who speaks the language of Dante."

I put the bundle inside the door. There was a living room, a bedroom, and a primitive kitchen. The walls were cracked and bare, and the plaster had long since fallen from the ceiling. The furniture was old but beautifully made, and everything was very clean. There was an odor of freshly washed linen. The mother led me to the divan in the living room. There was a portrait over it, done in oil by a good artist; it was at least fifty years old, and the man in it looked like the old lady.

She sat down next to me and folded her hands. "You must pardon the conditions under which we live," she said. "It is the war."

"I know," I said.

"This house was our property. We were so well off. Then came the bombardments, and..." she waved a hand. "*Grazie a Dio*, it is almost finished."

She was silent for a moment.

"Excuse me. I have forgotten the duties of a hostess. You like cognac?"

"No, *grazie*."

"Nonsense. All Americans like cognac. I am sorry I do not have any whisky, but I have some excellent cognac. It belonged to my family. Lydia!" she called.

The girl came in. She no longer wore the sweater over her dress, and her arms were wet, as though she'd had them in water.

"Give Tino some cognac," said her mother, "and be polite to our company. You are forgetting the manners I have taught you." She turned toward me. "Poor girl, she is always working."

Lydia poured something from a chipped decanter, set a single glass on a tray, and brought it over to me. Then she sat down on the chair opposite, crossing her legs. I looked at them.

"You don't drink with me?" I asked the mother.

She shook her head regretfully. "It is too strong for a woman. Do not be afraid, for it is good. Drink it."

I took the glass in my hand and tasted it. It was really excellent and of a fine, mellow quality. I told her so.

"This is the real thing," she said. "Not like what they sell today. What do you do in the Army, Tino?"

"I'm a Supply Sergeant," I said.

Lydia smiled. "It is a good position to have in Naples," she said. I didn't need any pictures to know what she meant.

"Maybe," I said. "But I don't need money that bad."

"He is right," said the mother. "The disgrace is not worth the money."

"Then you give presents to your girl friend," said Lydia.

"I have no girl friend," I said.

"Then you are a saint," said Lydia, "for in Naples all the Americans have girl friends. You do not look to me like a saint."

"No," I said. "I am no saint, but I have no girl friend."

"Tino," said the old lady gravely. "I am glad to hear you say that. You are perfectly right. Have nothing to do with the girls here. Try to remember, when you go home, that there are many poor but honest families who have starved in silence rather than eat in shame." She looked at her daughter. "It has been hard for us too, very hard. But we have kept our self-respect. I praise God that I have a daughter like her." Lydia was examining the palms of her hands.

"You should be proud of her," I said. "She is a fine girl."

Lydia raised her head and looked at me. The mother smiled.

"The Americans have all been kind to her," she said. "They have treated her like their sister. If it had not been for their kindnesses, we would have starved. Lydia had many friends, good boys. They would come up here in the evening and talk of their homes and their families, and bring us chocolate, and flour, and those rations in the cans that the soldiers have. There was Corporal...what was his name, Lydia?"

"I forget," said the girl. She looked down at the floor.

"How could you forget him, Lydia? He was so good to us. He used to come up here every night until his company moved from Naples. Giorgio, that was his name. He was very kind. They give us so many things and ask for nothing in return."

I set the glass down and stretched my legs, getting ready to leave.

"You will not have another?" asked the mother.

"No, *grazie*," I said.

Lydia got up and poured me another glass quickly. "Be still, and drink it," she said. "It will do you good."

"*Grazie.*" I drank it quickly, feeling the warmth spread through my body. It was beginning to go to my head. Lydia sat down opposite me again, and crossed her legs, as she had before. They were nice legs. They were very nice legs. She was a nice girl. What the hell, I thought.

I put the glass down decisively and stood up. "I really must be going," I said. My voice sounded strange in my ears.

"I will go down with you," said Lydia, getting up, "or you will lose your way."

"I'll be all right," I said.

"Nonsense," said the mother, "she always does that for our American friends." She walked with us to the door. "You will come again?"

"*Si, signora.* Thank you for the fine cognac. *Arrivederci.*"

"*Arrivederci.*"

Lydia walked ahead of me, silently, down the iron stairway to the second floor. My head was light, and the floor seemed to lift under the pressure of my feet. Lydia lit the candle as we descended below into the darkness. The shelter was very still. I could hear myself breathing, and was very conscious of Lydia and her clean white dress. We reached the shelter where the benches showed dimly in the candlelight. Suddenly Lydia stumbled as though she'd tripped, and fell against me with a little cry. I grabbed her arm about the elbow to keep her from falling, and the candle sputtered out as it dropped to the floor.

We were in absolute darkness. Lydia was soft and warm, and smelled of soap.

"I must have tripped," she said.

"Yes," I said. "Did you hurt yourself?"

"No." I still had her pressed against me. She made no effort to move. "It is very dark here," she said.

"Yes," I said. "Let's find the candle." I dropped her arm and went to the floor on my knees, exploring the surface until I felt the warm wax under my fingers. "Here it is," I said. "I have it."

There was a pause. "I have no more matches," she said.

"I have." I pulled a book of them from my pocket, struck one, and lit the candle. "We were lucky I had matches," I said. "Next time bring some with you."

"Yes," she said.

We climbed the ladder to street level.

"Thanks for showing me the way," I said. "Be careful going back."

"Yes. You will come to see us again?"

"Yes. *Arrivederci*, Lydia."

"*Arrivederci*." She looked as though she were going to say something else, but apparently changed her mind and walked abruptly away. I watched her legs disappear into the shadows.

What the hell, I told myself. You're imagining things. She's fifteen and she's a nice kid and has a nice mother.

And then I thought: but this is Naples in 1944 and she doesn't want to eat chestnuts. And she has nice legs.

I was still thinking about it when I got back to camp. I walked over to Luigi and looked up into his chipped stone face.

"*Signor*," I said, "you don't know the half of it."

(This story is taken from the author's autobiographical novel, *Nothing Will Ever Be the Same*, a work in progress.)

TIME-DEFYING PLACES
PATRICIA MATUSZEWSKI

Should you seek out these special places: On California's Central Coast, follow the Carmel Valley until it finally melts into the wider Salinas Valley. Take Hwy 101-S to Jolon Road and continue to Ft. Hunter Liggett and Mission San Antonio de Padua. Explore the mission, have lunch, and head coastward via Nacimiento-Ferguson Road (the Bended Sky Road), which crosses the Santa Lucias and joins the Coast Road south of Lucia. Highway 1 north up the Big Sur coast now seems like a very easy drive. At Highway 1 and Carmel Valley Road, some ten hours and 180 miles later, you will have come full circle.

> CARMEL VALLEY
> After the Village, the past.
> Lavender gold bouquets
> sweep misted hills
> and ancient homesteads
> on dappled river.
> Birdsong in stillness.
> Today, a century ago.

> JOLON
> Ghosts of history
> over Jolon
> in drowsing day
> and moonswept night.
> The forgotten ones
> walk these hills
> seeking Los Burros mines'
> golden promise.

SAN ANTONIO/HUNTER LIGGETT NAVAL AIR STATION

San Antonio de Padua
in a field of flowers,
a field of history,
a field of artillery.

For this Mission
shares space
with another might,
another power.

Separate and together.

SANTA LUCIAS TO BIG SUR

We follow ghosts
on El Camino Real,
ancient pathway
of ambered oak,
flowered fields,
and Bended Sky Road
to sun fogged coast.

Past and present, one.

IT'S ALL IN THE CARDS

KEN JONES

As they stared into the camera lens, he in his ill-fitting tuxedo and she in her scratchy lace veil, Larry and Rose's thoughts were far from those of other couples beginning a new life together. Their heads were full of a combination of bewilderment and dread. Understandable, given the fact they'd known each other less than an hour.

Two days previously Larry—who had been christened Javier twenty-three years earlier in the Southern California border town where he was born—sat in protective custody in the small Mexican village of El Pollo Muerto, high in the mountains above the Sea of Cortez. His protectors, a scruffy group of CIA field types, had the job of keeping him alive. At least until he could give testimony that would land an obscure but powerful drug lord, known as The Lizard, in a dusty prison cell to stay.

After his testimony, Javier had been unceremoniously handed off to a trio of dark suits with sunglasses who hustled his skinny, sweaty body onto a waiting helicopter for the trip north. While in the air, all traces of the man who had been Javier Rodriguez Gutierrez were obliterated. When the helicopter landed at a wind-blown field in west Texas, a brand new person, Larry Swift, stepped out into the hot afternoon sun.

* * *

While Larry nee Javier sweated out his testimony south of the border, Rose, or should I say Belle, found herself

66

being rushed from a burning apartment building in midtown Chicago. A bomb had just ripped through her father's penthouse apartment in a failed attempt to keep her sweet daddy from tying the final bow around the DA's case against suspected mob boss Guido Sarcosa. At the time of the blast, Belle's father Anthony Bentucci — ensconced aboard an unmarked Coast Guard gunship somewhere near the middle of Lake Michigan — had just made the prosecutor's day by providing over three hundred pages of deposition. Part of the deal was to keep his only daughter Belle out of harm's way, permanently.

Had she not been in the hallway outside the apartment, threatening the building superintendent for not fixing a leaky toilet, Belle would surely have been part of the debris slowly settling on the expensive cars parked on the street below. As it happened, three FBI agents had arrived to collect her at the very moment the bomb went off. In the confusion, they spirited her out of the building unseen and put her on a plane to Texas.

The following morning, the *Chicago Sun Times* would report the tragic death of Anthony Bentucci, one of the city's most respected construction contractors, and his beloved daughter Belle in a freak explosion at their midtown apartment. Authorities would point to a faulty gas line as the cause, and hint that a warrant was pending for the building owner's arrest.

* * *

Rose and Larry met for the first time in a convection oven of an office beside the main hangar at a Texas airfield. After being given a change of clothes and allowed to clean up some, they had been left alone in the small office. The two didn't speak, not knowing what role, if any, the other might play in their new identity. After a few nervous minutes spent looking at anything but each other and listening to the dull tick of the clock on the wall, they both jumped when the office door opened.

A man entered carrying two manila folders. His stained tie rested at half-mast and his forehead was as wrinkled as his sweat-soaked white shirt. "Welcome to your new life," he said, holding up the folders and sitting heavily on the corner of the desk. "These folders contain everything there is to know about the new you. Your new background, history...the whole story."

Larry and Rose stared blankly at the man, who rubbed the back of his neck and looked as if he'd rather be anywhere else on earth.

"The Federal Witness Protection Program's been under a lot of budget pressure lately," he said finally, almost apologetically. "The bean counters are all over us." He took a deep breath and studied the peeling paint on the ceiling for a second or two. "In order to make this thing work at all, we've created a new life for you two...ah, together."

Larry and Rose looked at each other now. In fact, they searched each other's eyes.

"What do you mean, 'together'?" Larry asked.

"Man and wife," the man answered. "You know, like a family?"

Larry reviewed his meager options. He knew if The Lizard's people found him, they wouldn't leave any pieces large enough to identify. He swallowed hard. His mouth suddenly felt as dry as the sand blowing past the office's dirty windows. He decided to keep his mouth shut.

Rose's mouth, however, dropped open. She knew her dad was safe for the time being, but if the Sarcosa clan ever suspected their bomb hadn't done the job...well, she didn't want to think about it. She fanned herself with a dog-eared copy of *Aviation Week*. "We got any choice in the matter?"

The man in the wrinkled shirt rubbed his stubbled chin and rechecked the ceiling. "Nope," he said. "For better or for worse, as the saying goes."

* * *

Two men in jeans and tee shirts helped the couple into theatrical wedding outfits, the backs open like hospital gowns.

They tied up the slack around Larry's bony frame and adjusted the straps to accommodate Rose's ample figure. When the couple looked like the real thing, the "newlyweds" were led into the hangar.

There, next to a flower and lace covered trellis and a painted sky backdrop, a bored looking sergeant in desert fatigues stood fiddling with his cable release. He positioned the two, mopped the sweat from their faces, and then rummaged in his duffel, finally pulling out a plastic bouquet. He fluffed up the sad little bundle and handed it to Rose. "Here hon, hang on to this. And for God's sake, try to smile."

The smell of fresh paint hung in the air and Larry could see the duct tape holding the fake flowers in place as the sergeant pushed and pulled at them and told them to hold still and smile. After several quick shots, he'd captured their blessed moment on film.

Blinking through spots in their eyes, the new couple – not married but looking that way – was hustled out of the hangar and onto a small jet for the flight to Monterey, California. As the sleek Gulfstream cruised smoothly toward the Peninsula, Larry and Rose thumbed through their folders. The FBI had been very thorough in creating their new life. All they had to do, it seemed, was live it.

A van waited on the tarmac when the jet rolled to a stop at the Monterey Airport. The couple was hurried into it and in less then fifteen minutes they pulled up in front of a modest house in the rolling hills above the city of Seaside, just east of Monterey. The driver carried the bags neither knew they had into the house and helped the two unpack, each into their own separate bedroom. When he'd finished, he handed Rose a card with a phone number and the words: *Federal Exterminators.* "Any problems," he said, "you call that number." He smiled, tipped his cap and left.

Larry rubbed his face tiredly and looked around the simply furnished living room. Sitting on top of the little upright piano in the corner, in a small grouping of FBI file pictures of grandmother and grandfather types, stood the bride and groom picture taken only hours ago in the sticky-hot Texas hangar. Larry walked over and picked it up. They looked younger, somehow; Rose was a little thinner, and Larry's bushy moustache had vanished. He shook his head and put the picture back on the piano.

He plinked a few keys. "Do you play?" he asked.

"No. And it's obvious you don't either."

Larry was about to reply when the sound of a dog whimpering came from the back of the house. They walked into the kitchen to investigate. A scrawny reddish pup wagged its entire body outside the sliding glass door leading to the back yard.

"What's the dog's name again?" Larry asked.

Rose referred to a laminated three-by-five card that she'd found with the information in her folder — sort of a pocket guide.

"Pal," she said. "Look at your card." She peered skeptically at the panting face staring lovingly from the other side of the glass. "He's kinda cute, I guess, in a strange sorta way. I wonder what his real name is."

Larry chuckled. "Hi there, Pal," he said, opening the door and kneeling to greet the eager mutt. It looked as if the dog had known them all its life. As Pal collected the scents, sounds and feels of his new parents, a woman's smiling face slowly appeared over the back fence.

"You must be the Swifts," she called. "Welcome to the neighborhood." She carefully lifted a homemade chocolate cake over the fence. It had a little metallic balloon stuck in the top with "Howdy Neighbor" printed on it. Larry took the cake from the woman and put it on the patio table.

"I'm Blanche," the woman said with a grin. "I know you two are busy now, but when you're all settled in we'll have time to get better acquainted. I just love your dog." She disappeared below the top of the fence.

Rose retrieved her purse from the kitchen counter and began to rummage through it. "God I could use a smoke," she said. "What did I do with my cigarettes?" Larry cleared his throat loudly, interrupting her frantic search. "What?" she said, looking up impatiently.

"You and I both quit two years ago," he said. He had a twinkle in his eye as he waved his laminated index card in the air. "Don't you remember?"

Rose made a sour face and muttered something in Italian that Larry didn't understand. She threw her purse on the counter as she strode back into the house.

Larry grabbed the cake and he and Pal followed her inside. "This cake looks pretty good," he said, "but I'm getting hungry for some real food." He opened the refrigerator door and peered inside. Rose began to open cupboards.

"Do you cook?" he asked finally, closing the refrigerator door empty handed.

Rose stood with her hands on her hips and looked around the kitchen. "Hell, I don't know," she said, throwing her arms in the air. "Let me check my card."

EARLY CHILDHOOD EDUCATION

MARTIN DODD

My warping began in the first grade. The first day, Mrs. Stietz announced that we would do finger-painting. I smeared a sky blue background on a sheet of paper. Then I made a series of tight spirals down the page, rather like Shirley Temple's curls (a predictable subject, as this was 1940). Mrs. Stietz raved about my art and tacked it up on the wall. Having achieved perfection, in the next finger-painting session I produced the same picture. This time there was no wall-hanging praise, merely a "very nice, dear, why don't you try something new?" Perfection seemed not to be a dependable target.

I don't know what wisdom can be drawn from this experience, except that *Stietz is German, this was 1940, and the Germans were in Paris.* The whole thing could have been a case of sabotage.

My values got totally distorted in the second grade. Mrs. Lawson gave us gold stars for every day we brushed our teeth—seven a week! At Faith Methodist Church, I got one gold star a week for attending Sunday School. There you have it—*seven stars to one*—avoiding cavities is seven times more important than staying out of Hell. It made sense to me. After one appointment for fillings, I knew that a dentist with a drill was at least seven times worse than the Devil armed only with a pitchfork.

While still in the second grade, I moved to a new home and a new school. My teacher was named Miss Mason, but two months before school was out, she became

Mrs. Bishop. Her names fit her perfectly. She had the personality of a brick and she issued assignments as if they came from God.

In the third grade, I had a reprieve. My teacher, Mrs. McCarty, was the single, real human being in the Atlanta school system. Under her, I learned the only truly useful stuff that has helped me ever since: the multiplication tables, short division, and that different birds have different songs. Thank you Mrs. Mac, wherever you are.

In the fourth grade, I returned to absurdity. Miss Daly was a white Watusi—six and a half feet tall. When she turned sideways, you couldn't see her. She was the tallest and skinniest person I had ever seen. Long division and geography, as mysterious as they were, could not overcome my awe of this female physical-spectacular. I continually tried to stand my #2 pencil on its point to understand how Miss Daly was able to stay upright. I never achieved it. She later became principal. Personally, I think she should have gone to the Smithsonian.

The fifth grade was the beginning of my twenty-year stint as a ne'er-do-well. Miss McBride had an Irish name like Mrs. McCarty from the third grade. However, the resemblance ended there. Miss McBride was not a real human being. She was, I am convinced, *Jesus in a skirt*. She was the personification of absolute grace. No matter how we behaved—like Dick and Jane or the Dead End Kids—she gave us candy. There was a *total disconnect* between behavior and reward. She was all Mercy and no Justice. This is not a good lesson for a pre-delinquent. I spent the next two decades trying to figure out why I got failing grades and pink slips instead of goodies.

Wrapped around my formal education was the realization that my sister was an only child. She got a clarinet, a piano, and lessons. Me? My grandfather taught me to play a Kleenex and comb. He called it a poor man's kazoo. I could live with that; it was the Ovaltine and the little redhead that got to me. My sister wanted a Little Orphan Annie Secret Decoder Ring. To get it, she had to send in the seals from the tops of at least a hundred and forty-seven jars. My mother was a waste-not, want-not kind of person. So, I drank a bathtub full of Ovaltine—my sister got the ring. Till this day, I cannot drink anything malt-flavored unless it's mixed with Prozac.

Soooo, those are some of my childhood lessons. What did I learn from all this?

Well, "as the twig is bent..." the ornament falls on the floor.

TO THE LEFT OF FOUNDER'S TREE, HUMBOLT STATE PARK
ILLIA THOMPSON

Heart burned out by long ago fires
hollowed redwood reaches above
grove companions.

Base gnarled and whorled,
elongated bark caresses
sturdy remains.

Gray weathered sinews,
burnished by filtered sun
lead to fresh growth on high.

Dark slender branches
hold pale green beginnings
...again.

~

MAGENTA
ILLIA THOMPSON

the shade of blood before it meets daylight
the juice of raspberries as tongue bursts flavor
the brightest stripe in a plaid back-to-school dress
late night jazz in a Parisian cafe
Chagall's "Lovers, A Study in Red"
Magenta, the color of a tear that will not fall

THE UNFAIR LABOR PRACTICE

PETER HOSS

Bozo burst into the union office. He was a florid, profane, long time organizer, veteran of many bitter battles. He was perpetually scowling. With Bozo the world was black and white. Management was black. The union was white. A second man in the office was Malapropos, who had worked his way up from the ranks by dogged persistence. Malapropos always managed to say the wrong thing at the wrong time. A third man was an aristocratic-looking young man with narrow rimmed glasses. Raised in a mainline Eastern suburb, he was the product of a prep school and Harvard. He had resolved to promote social justice by trying to help the lot of the workingman. His name was Algernon Reginald Buffington III, but everyone called him Ivy League.

Bozo growled, "You won't believe this. We found this vineyard owner who hired ten guys to work all day. Then he went out and found five other guys. Some worked six hours. Some worked four hours. Some only worked two hours. At the end of the day he paid them all the same. The guys who worked two hours got the same pay as the guys who worked eight hours. When the guys who worked longer complained, he told them that they had agreed to work for what he paid them, and that was it. He said it was his money and he could do it that way if he wanted. File an unfair labor practice against the son of a bitch."

Malapropos interjected, "It's the most unheard of thing I ever heard of."

"Did he pay union wages?" Ivy League asked.

"Well yeah, he did," said Bozo, "but so what?"

76

"Did he violate any union rules?" Ivy League asked.

Bozo responded. "I checked it out. The bastard looks clean. All reports are that he treats his workers very well. They speak highly of him. They say he is a model employer."

"He was handing out these," said Ivy League, pulling out a stack of tracts. "It is from the Bible, the Gospel of St Matthew, Chapter 20. The vineyard owner seems to be trying to follow this parable literally."

Bozo was fuming. "The bastard is up to no good. He's trying to bust the union. He'll bring in scabs, then fire the union members. Go after him. " He looked at Ivy League.

"I thought of that," said Ivy League, "but I looked at his record. He has no history of union busting. We cannot pre-judge. He has a contract that he has always honored."

"Maybe it is just sour grapes," said Malapropos.

"He didn't hire the workers out of the union hall," said Bozo. "Can't we get him for that?"

Ivy League was pensive. "I cannot see why he can't pay someone for more hours than they worked," he said. "After all, it is his money."

"I think it is a question of whose ox is being goosed," said Malapropos.

Bozo was still furious. "The son of a bitch is up to something, I know it," he said. "I may have to go over and slash his tires and put sand in his gas tank."

"I am puddled and befizzled. What does the tract say that he is handing out?" asked Malapropos.

Ivy League summarized the parable. "A vineyard owner hires workers at different times during the day and offers them a penny to work for him. They agree, then complain about the same pay for different hours worked. The vineyard owner tells the workers they agreed to the wages ahead of time, it is his money, and they have no right to complain. It is a parable, designed to illustrate the point made at the end that the first shall be last and the last shall be first, and that many are called and few are chosen."

This was too much for Malapropos to absorb at one time.

"Hold on," he said. "A penny a day is not union wages."

"There has been some inflation since this happened," Ivy League said.

"Well, everyone knows the first are first and the last are last," said Malapropos. "Who can argue about that?"

"He is talking about the kingdom of heaven, not the kingdom on earth," said Ivy League.

A faint recognition came to him of his youth as an altar boy in the most high church Anglican parish on the eastern seaboard, where the "frozen chosen" came to worship.

Bozo had been listening intently. His childhood flashed back to him, a devout Roman Catholic mother taking him to mass every Sunday in the impoverished neighborhood where he had grown up. Bozo had fallen away from the Church. He concluded that the management bastards had infiltrated the Church and taken it over because they had the money. He now regarded the Church as part of the enemy. However, he thought about the parable and entertained a thought. The thought was that the workers and the union were surely the last on earth but they would be the first in heaven, while the management bastards would be burning in hell. He was intrigued by this thought, but he was still mad and believed that the vineyard owner must be up to no good. He lashed out at the suggestion of Ivy League that the vineyard owner just might be acting from good motives.

Malapropos had been reflecting on what he heard. "So it's about the kingdom of heaven," he said. "Well, I'll be going to hell."

Ivy League looked at the veteran organizer and spoke with unaccustomed fervor.

"For Christ's sake, Bozo, have you become so cynical, dogmatic, closed-minded and mean-spirited that you cannot believe that an employer can act from decent motives?"

Bozo scowled. "You prep school candy ass," he said. "For Chrissakes, you don't understand the real world."

He was about to storm out of the office, but he stopped; his perpetual scowl softened, and an unaccustomed look of benevolence came over him.

"I'm sorry kid. You may have a point. You are down in this cesspool trying to do the right thing. I don't know why. If I had your connections, I wouldn't be in this shit pit. I'd be driving around in a Mercedes with a babe on each arm. But I got nowhere else to go."

Bozo paused. His eyes watered. "I've been doing this too long. See you later. Have a good night. Go get laid or something."

"I never saw him act like that. He must have loosed a screw," said Malapropos.

Ivy League returned to his cheap motel room and spent a sleepless night reflecting on Bozo's remarks. This was not really his world, he thought. He knew the meaning of the parable. He could not gain more of God's favor by working hard and doing good deeds. He was reminded of the parable of the talents, that he should do the most with what God had given him. He was in the wrong place. He decided to call the investment bank in New York that had offered him a job and see if the position was still open. He did and it was. He decided to return home.

Malapropos spent a sleepless night in a cheap motel pondering how the last could be first and the first could be last. Malapropos thought to himself, "I say so many stupid things, it's the only talent I have. Maybe I could be a stand-up comic and make people laugh." The idea appealed to him. Bozo spent a sleepless night in a cheap motel trying to figure out what kind of plot the vineyard owner was hatching, but the answer eluded him. He thought about what Ivy League had said. Maybe, just maybe, the vineyard owner was capable of doing a decent thing for his workers.

Maybe he was trying to prove a point. After all, he paid union wages and did not seem to be trying to cheat anyone. Those wanting more wages were wanting more than they bargained for. A deal is a deal. Maybe I ought to buy the bastard a beer, so as to get to know him better.

Ivy League told Bozo of his decision to return home. Bozo said it was a good idea.

"Can I come see you? Will you show me New York? I have always wanted to go there."

"Of course, I would love to see you and show you around."

They embraced as they parted.

Malapropos shared his idea about being a stand-up comic with Ivy League, who thought it was a great idea.

"But I don't know how to go about it."

"I know some agents," Ivy League said. "Come see me and I will introduce you."

Malapropos went to New York and Ivy League introduced him. Malapropos was an instant success as a stand-up comic. People rolled in the aisles. Malapropos never ran out of material. He appeared with Jay Leno, David Letterman and Garrison Keiler. He became wealthy.

Bozo remained curious about why the vineyard owner had decided to pay his workers in such a crazy way. He decided he would buy the vineyard owner a beer and ask him why. He did so. The vineyard owner was apprehensive at first, knowing Bozo by reputation, but they made some small talk and found out they both liked dogs, baseball, and country western music. The vineyard owner decided he could share openly with Bozo.

The vineyard owner explained, "I was on a business trip. I was staying in a hotel and I had nothing to do, so I picked up the Gideon Bible that was there and opened it to a page at random. I turned to Matthew 20 and read it. The sky lit up and I was temporarily blinded. I decided the message was intended for me, so I resolved that I would do exactly as the scripture directed."

"I'll be goddamned. You are legit after all. I was wrong about you." Bozo shook the hand of the vineyard owner. "But tell me," he asked, "how did it work out?"

"It did not work out at all," the vineyard owner said. "The next morning no one showed up for work at 7:00 a.m. and busses arrived at 3 p.m. from as far away as L.A. I had to go back to the old routine."

Bozo looked at the vineyard owner sympathetically.

"Yeah, I know," he said. "I know those guys. You give 'em an inch and the sons of bitches take a mile." Bozo continued, "Besides, the parable is about the kingdom in heaven, not the kingdom on earth. It means that in the kingdom of heaven the first shall be last and the last shall be first, and many will be called and few chosen." Bozo swelled with pride at this display of wisdom. Then the union organizer in him reasserted itself.

"If you really want to do something for your workers, you should make them do a full day's work and double their pay," he suggested.

"I never thought of it that way," the vineyard owner responded. "I know some kind of a message was being sent, but I didn't get it. I will try that."

The vineyard owner did as Bozo suggested and doubled the pay of his workers. The new experiment did not work. The bottom dropped out of the wine market and the vineyard owner could not compete because of his higher labor costs. The vineyard owner went broke. He concluded that Jesus never owned a working vineyard.

Bozo felt bad, and believed that he was responsible for the insolvency of his new friend. He decided to do something about it. He persuaded the workers to take stock in the vineyard for the wages the vineyard owner could not pay. He went into partnership with the vineyard owner, cashed in his union benefits and invested them in the vineyard, with he and the vineyard owner each sharing in majority ownership of stock. The vineyard was saved and everyone prospered, the vineyard owner, Bozo, and the workers. Sales of wine from the vineyard went from last to first within a year. Bozo was hailed as a genius and accepted by other vineyard owners, who were his former enemies. The perpetual scowl vanished and Bozo became known as "Smiley." Bozo and the vineyard owner adopted a new slogan: "An honest day's work for an honest day's pay."

Ivy League prospered in the investment banking business, utilizing his talents and connections. He became a multi-millionaire, but never lost his social conscience. He set up a foundation for educating children of impoverished vineyard workers and built health clinics for the vineyard workers and their families.

Bozo (aka Smiley), Malapropos and the vineyard owner became trustees of the foundation set up by Ivy League and traveled to New York for meetings. Bozo (aka Smiley) bought a Mercedes and dated beautiful women. The last beautiful date became his first and only wife.

As Bozo described it, "Though many were called, only one was chosen."

AND SPRING IS HERE
HELEN OLSON

Buried under the shroud of ugly, hateful rubble
My omniscient spirit finds its likeness.
The cacophony of steely cold madness
Cannot always breathe freely,
Will not go uninterrupted by the unending flame of desire.
And Spring is here.
Disease does harness the innocent body
And threaten the vulnerable spirit.
The soul must forever reach for the warmth of the sun.
It is there in eyes, voices and touch.
Spring is here.
Spring is here in this flower, and in this Life.
Winter shall be abated again and again
By reason most divine.
See the golden poppies, the shades of green far too many
to count.
Float above and into the gentle folds
Of eternal loveliness.
Know it, hold it close, and forever believe.
Believe, for Spring is here.

ON CONSERVATION AND ENJOYMENT
HELEN OLSON

A bird must flap its wings
Before it can soar
And when it soars
It does not waste energy,
Or contentment
Flapping its wings.
Why do I always flap my wings
Even when I begin to soar?

A WEATHERED VIEW
THROUGH WINDOW PANES
ILLIA THOMPSON

inside protected place of home
white walls embrace quiet

colors weave to please the eye
textures liven at the touch

time flows liquid lullaby
story accompanies memory

outside tumble of wind
rain slants music on the roof

after the storm
shadow and sun play tag

no one wins

~

MEMORIAL TO MOTHER
ILLIA THOMPSON

Over two years since I held your soft hand
and thanked you for deep friendship.
I miss your delight, feel older without you.

My matriarchy slips and slides,
the seams not taut, its length a bit askew
as I meet your phantom presence.

Your crystal essence fractures time,
my pen becomes the lips to brush
a kiss upon your brow.

AMANDA

WALTER E. GOURLAY

When I told Julie, my girl friend, that I'd been accepted at Graduate School in Cambridge, Mass., her reaction was predictable.

"I'm going with you." Although she could, and usually did, talk and talk and talk, she could also use short, declarative sentences when she'd made up her mind about something.

"What about your job?" I asked.

"A receptionist? I can find that anywhere. Besides, I only work part-time anyway. What is it," she said, searching my face, "don't you want me up there with you? I promise you I won't get in your way. I'll get my own apartment and we'll go on just as we do here in New York."

And so it was settled. That's the kind of relationship we had, easy and non-possessive. Mostly.

A few days after I moved into the graduate dormitory and classes began, she took the Greyhound to Boston, lugging the two big suitcases that held all her worldly goods, and began the hunt for a place to live. She'd been to Boston once before, on a bus tour. She loved places with charm and history, and she'd felt this was her city.

"I've found just the place," she told me, the day after she arrived. "A furnished studio on Beacon Hill. A bit small but with atmosphere. Come look at it."

It was on the third floor, really the garret of an old red brick building that must have dated from the early 1800's. It overlooked Revere Street, narrow, short and paved with brick, opening at one end on historic and aristocratic Louisburg Square at the summit of Beacon Hill. In the other direction it descended to busy, lively Charles Street, with coffee shops, restaurants and public transportation. "Just like the Village," she declared. "Except not so many crazies."

The building had charm, although in the winter the sidewalks and the street were perpetually glazed with ice and hard-packed dirty snow. In the spring heaps of slushy mush mixed with the ashes and gravel that Boston, that most traditional of cities, pretended was a snow removal system.

Julie's studio, tucked in under the eaves, was a tiny sitting room with a turn-of-the-century bathroom, an electric hotplate, and an alcove with a queen-size bed covered with a large down filled hand-made quilt, patterned in white and red roses. When I stayed overnight, I had to bend at the waist in order not to hit my head when I stood in the alcove. The dresser and the rest of the furniture looked like the gleanings from rummage sales over the years.

Julie, I knew, would be happy there. A native of San Francisco, where history seemed to begin with the earthquake of 1906, she was fascinated by what Californians called "Back East." She was especially entranced by New England, where, according to her Californian grasp of history, the entire American Revolution had taken place. Except for Virginia, of course, where the British surrendered, after having been driven out of Boston by the Minutemen. It had taken me some time to disabuse her of the notion that Washington had crossed the Delaware somewhere in New England, or that Pennsylvania was next to Massachusetts. She never did quite accept the fact that New York State had taken part in the Revolution too.

Anyhow, one day in early winter she informed me that she hadn't slept well the night before, nor on any other night recently when I was absent. "No," she said, "don't flatter yourself. It's nothing to do with you. It's about someone else. Or some*thing* else." Her jaw tightened, as though indignant.

"It's a young woman," she said. "She comes in the middle of the night. She comes in and opens and closes the drawers of my dresser, as though she's looking for something. It wakes me up."

I stood silent.

Julie rattled on. "She's a young woman, kind of pretty. Maybe about eighteen or nineteen. Very pale and thin, as though she's been sick for a long time. Long, loose, blonde hair and wears a thin white nightgown."

"Do you talk to her?"

"She doesn't hear me. When I sit up to get out of bed, the woman disappears. Like smoke."

I put my arm around her. "A bad dream," I said.

"No," she answered. "She's looking for something. I wish I knew what it is. She doesn't come when you're around."

"Maybe she doesn't like men," I suggested.

Julie shrugged. "Probably with good reason," she said. "She'd be very pretty, if only she didn't look so pale and thin."

I knew what was coming. Whenever anything really bothered Julie, I was supposed to fix it or tell her what to do. The way Julie saw the world, that's what men are for.

"I have no experience at laying ghosts," I said, "if you'll pardon the expression. As a matter of fact, I've never met one or wanted to meet one. I don't even believe in them."

"As for laying ghosts," she answered, "I'm glad to know you draw the line somewhere."

Then she turned serious. "I don't believe in ghosts either," she said. "That stuff is nonsense. Everything that people call supernatural has a perfectly natural explanation. It's all connected to energy. Past events and even future events make waves of energy that sometimes become attached to a particular place. Like this room. If we understood time and energy better, we could explain all that superstitious junk. Some people, like me, are just receptive to such signals, and others—like you—aren't, or at least you don't admit it."

I could sense a long lecture coming. Julie had a theory about everything, and once she started on a topic, she could discourse for hours. She was very lovable but sometimes unbearable. I cut her short. "So what do you want me to do?"

"I want you to help me move all this furniture to find out what she's looking for."

"And if we don't find it?"

"Then I'll have to find another apartment. Or else you'll have to move in with me." She smiled to let me know she was joking. "There's something here. There has to be."

It didn't really take us long. Under the bed, buried in the dust and lint of decades of indifferent housekeeping, I found it—a white comb beautifully carved out of ivory or whalebone. On the long handle were the initials, "A.S." in a cursive script.

"Alice," I said. "Maybe Amanda. I bet its Amanda." I offered it to her.

Julie grimaced. "Take it," she said. "Take it downstairs and throw it in the trashcan. I don't want her here hunting for it."

"It's a beautiful comb," I said. "A real antique. Maybe a gift from her lover."

"Get rid of it. I don't want her coming back. The comb brings her here. I need my eight hours of sleep."

I looked out the window. The first snowfall of the year, mixed with sleet, had begun. Typical Boston weather.

"Throw it in the trash can," Julie insisted. "Let her find it there."

I had a vision of poor, pretty Amanda, sick and wearing only a thin, transparent nightgown, out in the sleet, searching through the trashcan. "She'll catch her death of cold," I said.

Julie looked at me as though I were crazy. "She's only a ghost," she said. "She can't die. Anyhow, I don't believe in ghosts. And neither do you. Right?"

"Right. But where will she go?" I asked.

"Anywhere but here. "

I went out in the bitter cold and did as Julie suggested, apologizing silently to Amanda. At first I thought of just placing the comb on the cover of the trashcan, to make things easier for her, but then I worried that someone could come along and steal it. So I dropped it in with the other trash, and replaced the cover.

That night, while sleeping next to Julie, I suddenly woke up. I definitely had the feeling that someone was in the room. I got gooseflesh on my legs and arms. I turned on the light. No one. Julie was now awake. "What is it?" she asked.

"I thought I heard someone in the room," I said.

"That's just the sound of snow hitting the window."

Eventually I went back to sleep. The next morning, as I trudged through the snow, I looked toward the trashcan to see if it had been disturbed. I was tempted to lift the cover and see if the comb was still there. But I didn't. After all, I don't believe in ghosts.

Amanda never bothered Julie again. But I still feel sorry for having forced her out into that cruel, cold night wearing only a flimsy nightgown. I wonder where she went.

WINTER DAY
LYNDA SPERRY JARDINE

Winter's landscape races down steep hillsides
Wearing its sparse robe of gray native grasses
A soft, faded cloak, flowing,
Plunging into shadowed canyons
There, pinned solid by clinging oaks,
Roots pierce deeply to bedrock.

~

THE STORM
LYNDA SPERRY JARDINE

The storm by dawn exhausted,
Its testament of chaos and wetness left
    everywhere.
In dark hidden places frost
Like a secret discovered by morning sun
Emerges as mist from soaked earth
Hovers gently against
Pristine brilliance of
Awakening sky.

THIS IS YOUR LAST CHANCE

PATRICIA MATUSZEWSKI

The day God spoke to him, Jim was thirty-two.

He sat slumped against a dying maple, holding up a shaking hand to shade his eyes against the opalescent glare of an overcast day as he stared across wind-blown litter. A dozen men sprawled on wooden park benches, newspapers covering their faces, thin gray shelter-blankets pulled up to their chins. *Where am I?* A fine drizzle had soaked him. He hunched his shoulders, shivering. *Is it dawn or dusk?* He looked down and saw his gray hooded Mariners sweatshirt from Goodwill was covered with mud and his jeans were torn at both knees. There was a rusty stain on his right thigh. *What had happened?* He touched his hair and beard — matted, wet — and pulled his hand away red-stained. His front teeth felt loose. *My head is killing me. How'd I get this lump? Can't seem to focus, dizzy, seeing double.* He picked up a bottle-shaped paper bag near his feet, tipped it up, found it empty, cursed, and tossed it aside.

He pulled himself up slowly, the pain in his thigh nearly causing him to pass out. He limped slowly to the bushes to take a leak, and then began to look for Bud and Herbie. The three of them had been hanging together for months now after that freakin' night at the homeless shelter. If they stuck together, they were all a lot safer. *Maybe they went back to the shelter. Nah, they wouldn't do that. Wouldn't just abandon me. We're the three musketeers, one for all and all that. They must be around.*

"Shoo, git," he said to a crow pecking at a sandwich still partly in its cellophane wrapper. He picked it up and walked back to the maple. *What is going on?* He had been high, in one way or another, all his life, and had awakened to many hangovers, but he could tell they were getting worse each time.

91

Bad enough to really worry him. Bad enough to make him think of taking the advice of the shelter chaplain to get sober and get out of Seattle—his land of temptation.

His school days had been littered with "Jim, *please*...sit down, be quiet, not now, wait your turn, give someone else a chance, slow down, calmly, if you'd only use some care, finish what you start, look out, be careful, and just once in your life, do as you're told," amid visits to the principal's office and calls to his parents. He was just wired wrong, mind throttle to the floor. Compulsive talking and frenetic activity burned off anxiety and nervous energy, but didn't make him many friends.

He self-medicated—alcohol, cigarettes, marijuana, and anything else that would slow his restless brain a bit or make him less aware of it. He couldn't stand the anxiety when he wasn't under the influence and he couldn't function when he was. Jobs and friends slipped away. His parents waited for the knock on their door in the middle of the night. He left Olympia, where he grew up, and wandered the skid rows of the Northwest.

Jim leaned back against the rough bark of the maple, felt the soft dampness of moss, heard crows disputing overhead. Their cawing reminded him of the sandwich—ham and cheese. Didn't seem to be spoiled. He was slowly coming out of his latest oblivion with the worst pain, headache, achy body, and sore, scratchy throat he'd ever had. *I need help, but first I need a drink bad. Wonder if any of those guys over there have anything hidden? I'll get that stick and...*

"THIS IS YOUR LAST CHANCE." He jumped and looked wildly around. There was no one close to him. It sounded like it came from above. He looked up. Nothing. Sometimes he heard things nobody had said. *Did I really hear it? Like old Chaplain Josef with a deeper voice. Why did he have to show me those disgusting pictures of Annie of Iowa and Lonnie from Louisiana, and Bill-John from Arkansas, all with the DT's—the "shaking crazies" Bud called it? Delirium tremens. I don't want to die like my old man did, or half the men in the family, the ones who didn't die of cirrhosis of the liver. I feel yellow today.*

A few minutes later, just when he decided maybe he had imagined it, he heard, very clearly, "**THIS IS YOUR LAST CHANCE.**"

The words sizzled like an electric current through every nerve and cell and body part. He froze, then he tried to scramble up, but couldn't stand. He just sat staring up at the tree. *If I get out of this, I'll start over. I swear. Just let me be able to walk again.*

One of the winos was starting to stir. Jim crawled over to him and asked, "You hear anything just now?"

The man didn't even look up, just reached a liver-spotted hand up, pulled the blanket over his head, and muttered in a raspy voice, "Like what?"

"Like a big voice."

"Didn't hear nothing. Don't hear so good any more. Anyway, I was asleep."

Jim fumbled in his pocket, found a few crumpled dollar bills, and quickly shoved them back, out of sight. *It's got to my brain, DTs of the brain. I have to get out of here, get help. Get away. Go home.*

"Where am I anyway?" he asked.

The old man pulled the blanket back a bit, shielded his eyes with his hand, looked up blearily, and gummed out the answer around his three remaining teeth, "New York."

"C'mon, where am I?"

The man looked more carefully at him, assessing the danger level, then muttered, "Same's last night, Seattle."

"Where's the bus station?"

The man yawned and waved his hand vaguely. "Down the hill four-five blocks, straight ahead."

Three hours later, Jim was back in Olympia. It had been years since he had been in church, but it seemed the thing to do. Besides, it provided meals and blankets.

The minister remembered him and urged, "Jim, come to one of our AA meetings. Give it a try. Just come one time."

He did. *This is my last chance* he told himself.

Two years later, after climbing on the wagon and falling off, he was sober. Now what? How in the world was he going to fill his time? *If I can't find something, I'm afraid of what I'll do. I'm all fizzed up inside like a can of soda that's just been shook, ready to explode.*

When the minister asked him to volunteer for missionary service in the Philippines, Jim was relieved to have something to do. Not that he was even sure where the Philippines were, but — *Why not? It's a free trip. Chance to see where the old man was in the war. It's not like I have anything else to do. It'll keep me away from the booze and pills and all. I crave stuff so bad when I'm anxious, and here I'm always anxious. Gotta get away.*

He asked what the most remote island was and volunteered to go there.

On the islands he found people so desperately needy, he made a difference in only a few weeks. *When did I last make a positive difference to anyone?* Suddenly, his energy level and reckless enthusiasm were assets. Since the villagers didn't understand what he was saying anyhow, no one cared how much he talked. They liked his friendliness and appreciated his interest in learning their language.

Finally his life had a purpose. Over the next decade, Jim started dozens of new missions. His work was well known in missionary circles and so was the miracle of his recovery. He told his story many times, always ending with "...how could I ignore the voice of God?"

Then, while on a world speaking tour, Jim returned to his old church in Olympia. When introducing him, Pastor Wendt spoke of the thirty missions Jim had sponsored and now oversaw; of the home mission in Manila where Jim and his wife Ami, a fellow pastor, raised their three children and ministered to two hundred forty street children, feeding, educating, and mentoring them; and of the books, the seminars, the many ways Jim and Ami helped others who want to create similar missions.

After Jim's talk, just as the food appeared, he noticed one of the homeless men in the cafeteria line looked familiar, something about the odd way he held his head like someone had given it a good twist and it hadn't gotten back to the start. By golly, it was Bud! *Amazing,* Jim thought, *he looks pretty much the same, just more used. Wonder if he'll recognize me?*

He crossed the room and said, "Hey Bud, remember me, Jim Kelley, from way back when?"

Bud looked up, momentarily confused, then brightened. "Jimbo, man, wow, didn't recognize you. Boy, do you look different! Lost the hair, put on weight, pretty upright looking now. I always wondered what happened to you. You just sorta disappeared. I guess we did too. Herbie and me went to Portland. Just came back a couple weeks ago."

"I woke up one day and you were gone."

"After doing that electronics store, it got too hot in Seattle and we figured to put some mileage on. I'm clean now and time's up, so I'm back. I've wondered sometimes, though, what happened to you after we dumped you."

"What you do mean, dumped me?"

"Uh, well... it was kind of a practical joke. We took you out to Orca Park and left you there. We were plenty sick of you by then. For weeks you'd been spouting the Bible non-stop—Abraham, Isaac, Matthew, Mark, and John. You just wouldn't shut up."

"I don't remember doing that."

"Surprised you remember any of it. You were real doped up those days. You were something else. Your mouth'd get going and you just wouldn't stop. You drove us nuts. I'm surprised somebody didn't stick a knife in your gizzard. Anyway, we decided to leave you in Seattle. You were fixin' to get us all busted. We put a few dollars in your pocket so you could get home, at least if you didn't get rolled. Herbie was feeling creative though. 'The jerk's been spouting so much Bible, let's give him something to talk about,' he said."

"What do you mean, something to talk about?"

Bud gazed around the room and nodded to a man in the corner, his attention momentarily distracted, then said, "You remember Herbie, don't you?"

"Sure. Kinda geeky, knew all about how things work."

"He's dead, OD'd. Well, he fixed up one of the tape recorders we stole so's it would keep playing and put it up in the tree we propped you up against. See, Herbie figured since you had been giving us the word of God, he ought to give you some of the same. He recorded several messages and we liked

"This is your last chance" or something like that, the best. It sounded good, kinda threatening."

Jim was staring, open-mouthed, face flushed. "That was a recording? A recording...! No, it couldn't be. I looked all over, everywhere, even up in the tree. I didn't see anything."

"You heard it, huh?"

Jim felt disoriented, as if watching all this from out of his body. *My whole life for the past ten years has been built on that moment of truth. Now he's saying it was a practical joke!*

"You ain't mad are you? We just wanted to scare you a little."

Jim was quiet for a moment until he regained his focus. He swallowed, put his hand on Bud's shoulder, and said, "You scared me a lot. Do you mind if I call you 'Prophet'?"

THE FLOOZY, THE FRUMP
AND FRED

JOY WARE

"How long do you think this'll last?" I asked Joanna. I had a vested interest in who our new Job Developer would be, but hated to miss the lovely day outside.

"There are five candidates," she replied.

"Well, I hope one of them fits. We sure need help."

Joanna and I were in the parlor of an ornate Victorian that had seen better days. The Private Industry Council rented this grand old lady for us, and we loved it in spite of its squeaking floorboards. Four of us, Joanna Green, Bill Hornet, our boss and fearless leader, and Melanie Ort, our financial officer and I sat at a formerly elegant but now badly scarred conference table. I read the names of the candidates scheduled for interviews this sparkling afternoon on the Monterey Peninsula.

"I hope we can find the right person to help us," I sighed as I glanced through the names.

"One candidate's listed twice," I noted gratefully. "We might get into the sunshine yet."

"No such luck," Joanna responded. "In addition to the three men, *two* women named Grayson are seated in the front room."

"That's weird. What's the connection, do we know?"

"Not sure. One shows 'single mom with three children,' the other states 'married with three stepchildren.' The two addresses are both near the high school."

"How about bringing in the first candidate and we'll find out?" Bill directed.

"Yes sir," I said as I walked out to where the applicants

were sitting in overstuffed armchairs scattered around the Victorian's front room.

"Annabel Grayson," I announced.

A woman with flaming red hair and an abundance of cherry makeup stood up, greeting me with an energetic "Good afternoon." She followed me back to the conference table. Her short skirt and low-cut ruffled blouse did their valiant best to hide the extra pounds around her middle.

The exuberant Mrs. Annabel Grayson was in that indeterminate range where it was exceedingly difficult to hazard a guess as to age. Was she 40, 55 even? I indicated a chair for her at the end of the table, then sat next to Joanna.

"Good afternoon, Mrs. Grayson, I'm Bill Hornet, General Manager, this is Melanie Ort, our Finance Officer. Alice Markham guided you in, and this is Joanna Green. Joanna and Alice are the two who need another Job Developer to help them meet the increasing caseload."

"Mrs. Grayson," Melanie began, "would you tell us please why you are applying for this position?"

"Call me Annabel, please," she smiled, her relaxed manner infectious.

"I've lived on the Peninsula for years, and have a lot of contacts through my work with the Non–Profit Exchange Board. I believe those contacts can lead to job training and even job shadowing. My skills will transfer quite easily."

"That's an interesting perspective, Mrs. Grayson—er, Annabel. We've never worked with the non-profit organizations, but they could be a good source of training for certain kinds of clients." Bill seemed impressed by her positive attitude and originality.

Melanie, her eyes on the interview list, called her Dorette, in error.

"No, that's his current wife. I'm the ex-Mrs. Grayson. I was married to Fred for nine years, though," Annabel added with a faint smile. "He's a nice man, I just couldn't stand being home alone. I thought he was a workaholic. I have to admit, however, he and Dorette are better together most of the time than Fred and I ever were. That's a fact. And, Dorette's been an absolute blessing as far as our kids go."

Dumbfounded glances bounced around the table. A wife and ex-wife on speaking terms? They'd applied for the same job? They lived in the same neighborhood? They agree on child rearing? What indeed is this Mr. Fred Grayson like? A regular mystery man, I thought, looking at the surprised faces around the conference table. Even with the motes dancing in the sunlight, it didn't feel like it would be all that tedious an afternoon.

"I've never found jobs for people," Annabel told us, "but I've sure raised a lot of money and filled volunteer positions for the Non-Profit Exchange Board."

We listened while she enthusiastically recited the highlights of four decades dedicated to various career tasks. Her skills, experience and flair would be valuable to us, but how old was this woman, I wondered? It was a question we weren't allowed to pose.

"Thank you Annabel. When we've reached a decision, you'll be contacted," Bill told her. I ushered her out.

The next three interviewees were escorted out as quickly as they were brought in. None of them could demonstrate experience in sales or had histories that included working well with people, essential skills for any Job Developer. Each was excused with Bill's, "You'll be notified when a decision has been reached."

That brought us to the second Mrs. Grayson. I walked out to the front room as her cell phone slid into her purse. Dorette stood, mumbled "Good afternoon" and kept her head lowered as she moved down the hall. She wore a mousy, nondescript gray skirt and sweater. Wisps of errant brownish hair escaped what was supposed to be a severe bun at the nape of her rather long neck. Her face was totally devoid of make-up. She seemed a polar opposite to the vivacious Annabel. How was it possible for the same man to have been married to both of these women, I mused, guiding her to her place at the table, thoroughly intrigued.

After the preliminaries Joanna asked, "Dorette, what experience do you have in sales?"

"Annabel would be much better in this job than I," came the reply.

Dorette's replies to the next three questions were an echo: "Annabel would be much better in this job than I."

Exasperated, I asked, "Dorette, why exactly have you applied to work as a Job Developer?" I heard the uncontrolled edge to my voice.

Before she could respond, there was a quick, sharp rap on the door, and a man wearing hospital whites burst upon us.

Dorette jumped up. "At last! Dr. Greenwood, I was afraid you'd be late," she exclaimed. "I want to go now, but I did it. I even answered some questions!" She beamed absolute triumph.

"Dorette's one of our outpatients," the doctor explained. "We've been successfully treating her for agoraphobia, haven't we, Dorette?" His smile was indulgent. "We're rather grateful for cell phones too, aren't we Dorette? This is our experimental therapy. Dorette makes appointments, then calls to tell me where and when to pick her up before she's reached an unacceptable stress level that could cause a relapse to her reclusive behavior." His smile was almost smug. "So far, our special brand of therapy has worked quite well." He then took her by the elbow and escorted her out of the room.

We were all but undone. It was a good thing that was the last interview, anyway. Bill and Melanie shook their heads in disbelief. Dorette's malady *was* sad, but Joanna and I burst into a fit of the giggles. We had to admit it certainly hadn't been a boring afternoon, with or without access to the sunshiny day.

Following a week's deliberation, we accepted the fact that Annabel Grayson had the talent and experience we sought. Despite her exuberant, slightly floozy appearance, she would bring a definite flair and terrific contacts to our work.

Over lunch on Thursdays I discovered the makings of a novel hidden in their stories. Dorette sometimes joined us, occasionally feeling compelled to whisper "Dr. Greenwood" into her cell phone. He'd appear and off she'd go.

Annabel had explained why she'd left Fred and opted for joint custody. "Living apart from a workaholic appeared less stressful than being home alone with three kids anyway," she'd told me. "Besides, I still have weekly interaction with my kids. They're teenagers and the arrangement works for everyone."

As for Dorette, she and Fred had met on a business trip to New York City when they were both attending the same Public Health convention. It was love at first sight for both of them, and luckily Fred was sympathetic and understanding when it came to his second wife's phobia.

Though I didn't understand it, I realized that these two women and a father had learned how to put their love and concern for the children ahead of themselves. They have been able to be consistent in their expectations and support of them.

Annabel and Dorette, I discovered, were actually very much alike. It was obvious to me they enjoyed many of the same interests.

Just a few weeks ago Dorette told me about her illness. "When I began to have panic attacks in the middle of a store, it was Annabel who'd come get me and take me home. She seemed to know just how trapped and scared I felt. For months, she rearranged her schedule to go with me when I just HAD to leave the house. She's been so good to me, you'd think she was a sister."

"But Dorette, you seem to be mostly okay now, thanks to Dr. Greenwood's cell phone therapy," Annabelle chimed in.

"That's for sure," replied Dorette. "It's good to have my life back!"

Dorette's transformation seemed to be complete the day she sat in our lunch room, tuna sandwich in hand, wearing a brilliant blue outfit, her hair in an elegant upsweep, make-up only slightly less subdued than Annabel's, regaling us with one of her escapades. There was very little of the frumpy, frightened Mrs. Grayson in this poised and lively lady.

Annabelle certainly wasn't the vamp I'd judged her to be, Dorette had emerged from a terrible disorder, and Fred — well, Fred just loved them both in his own way.

THE HUNT

MARTIN DODD

It was cold. He bent over, gripping a bag tight with the open end held low and wide between clenched fists. He squinted steadily at the space between the house and the fence that separated yards. *That's where they'll come,* he thought. *The guys'll run them down between the fence and the house.* He brought his shoulder against his cheek and wiped his runny nose on the sleeve of his corduroy jacket, but he didn't take his eyes off the spot.

They all had agreed that he was to be the key man — the catcher. The others would be bush-beaters. He could hear them, out front, yelling, doing their part. He could imagine them with sticks, hitting bushes, raking under them. *I'll show 'em I can do my part.*

Things would be different after this. Once, he had cried when hurt playing touch football. After that, the other boys usually left him out, or teased him. They had even "pantsed" him in front of girls. He had tried to hide, but embarrassed and confused, he pulled one leg out and ran, dragging his pants behind the other leg. The girls still giggled when they saw him. He couldn't stand any more teasing. Now things were going to change.

He couldn't hear the others anymore. *Maybe shoutin' didn't get 'em. Maybe they're sneaking up on 'em now.* One of the guys had said, "They're kinda like quail. You don't see 'em. They blend in with the grass and bushes, but they're here, okay."

They got wings, maybe flap like chickens. Not fly, just hop higher. Imagining a bird running toward the space between his

102

legs while another flapped and hopped, he waved the bag up catching one and then down bagging the imaginary runner. "Gotcha, gotcha."

The December sun was low. He shivered and wiped his nose on his sleeve again. He was ready. *Things'll be different now.* It was quiet. His eyes were slits, and his knuckles were white. He whispered his determination: "By God, I'll bag any ol' snipe they drive my way — I'm the catcher."

S+

ILLIA THOMPSON

A two-inch square of yellowed paper with faint writing falls from her maroon velvet-lined jewelry box, and she remembers...

Ruth, dark-haired and wide-eyed, loved language. She rolled it around on her tongue and tossed it about in her mind, but only shyly spoke it. On paper her phrases fell like waterfalls, delighting her in their music as words became silent playthings.

During Ruth's junior year in high school she walked, counting to herself. "One, two, three, four...eight," the long blocks toward school, her daily destination. Each class ticked slowly by, minutes stacked upon minutes until the pile reached fifty, allowing release and the procession into the next class.

Mr. Calitri's class, so different. There, Ruth wished time would stop as she sat alert and let her eyes follow Mr. Calitri, absorbing his dark eyes and classic good looks while letting his deep voice stir her imagination. Macbeth came to life. Poe's desperate pathos throbbed. Emily Dickinson's words became hers. At home Ruth labored over assignments, then turned them in written in her finest handwriting. She anxiously awaited comments upon their return. "Good work, keep on." "You have talent." "Exceptional quality." Although she blushed as she read these, she kept on and found an awakening of courage. At last, a place that felt at home, at school.

The first report card carried the mark of *S* or *U*, for satisfactory or unsatisfactory, for students in all classes. Mr. Calitri placed an *S* on that blue card, and on her white makeshift book cover he wrote *S+.* That's how the carefully cut out square ended up in Ruth's jewelry box.

All semester Ruth's work flourished. Mr. Calitri seemed to look especially her way while he taught. He encouraged her to join *Forest Leaves*, the school's literary magazine.

Summer vacation found Ruth writing poetry and stories. She placed each finished piece in a large white envelope with Mr. Calitri's name written neatly across the front.

Summer ended and Ruth's senior year began. She now could use the central senior marble staircase. She applied to colleges. She was a writer.

A few weeks into the semester, Ruth took the white envelope to school. She waited patiently, her heart pounding, outside Mr. Calitri's room.

He almost ran into her on his way out. "Excuse me," he said in an offhand manner. "Oh, you were in my class last year, weren't you? Now, what's your name? Something from the Bible, I think."

She stared at him. Nodded. Slowly she walked to the bustling cafeteria for lunch. That evening, she placed the white envelope in the back of her bottom desk drawer.

THE AD

HAROLD E. GRICE

I skim through the paper. Get to the classified personals. My eye stops on a small, direct, no kidding around, clearly expressed ad.

God, I wish I'd written that! It's not often you see an ad that clear.

Ads. How interesting it must be to develop the usable ad. A lot of them use gimmicks and/or a near-naked lady to grab attention. Anytime I see a naked lady in an ad, I pass on by. Naked ladies get my attention only when they are warm and smell nice.

But thinking of ladies, I remember playing cards in the Tonopah Casino in Nevada. I wasn't paying much attention until they changed dealers. Suddenly those hands manipulating the cards were long, slender, and very dexterous.

Those hands were mesmerizing.

Those hands would look great in one of those glossies, with gloves, rings, fingernail polish, whatever – as long as the hands were positioned to show the dexterity and grace of them. Finally, I looked up. The lady was young and slender all over. Well, nearly all over.

But, to get back to the ad.

It was direct, clear and positive. Why can't all ads be that way?

While watching a TV ad, I see an image for the count of 1,2,3,4 seconds, then it's gone. New image: 1, 2, 3, 4, 5 seconds, then it's gone. Another: 1,2,3 seconds, gone. The idea is to give the mind an image without definition exactly, but with a name.

People get paid big bucks to do this. It is a strange world.

Now this ad I admire. I read it again. I want to respond. I cannot imagine the person in this ad, and it would be damned interesting to find out. But I don't think I qualify.

That probably has to do with growing up a country boy, and guitars, and cowboys and fast cars.

Thinking of qualifying, you ever respond to one of those ads about "call and get your free – etc." whatever? I did this once. It was a free investment digest or some such. No obligation or requirement, etc., etc., etc. I responded and mailed in the card.

Some guy called wanting to discuss my financial needs, expectations, etc. After I realized what he was carrying on about, I said, "The ad said no obligation. This investment digest will be yours free with no obligation."

He came back with, "What, are you stupid? Some sort of dummy? That ain't the way it works. There is always a follow up. What else did they teach in kindergarten this morning?" And then he slammed the phone down. Jeez! Such salesmanship.

That's probably why I like this ad. Either you got it or you don't.

Yeah, what an ad. Wish I'd written it. Now I gotta call. Well, maybe I will. I don't know.

Let's see, read it again. Do I qualify?

It reads: "*You got the money, honey, I got the time.*"

THE WINDFALL

GEORGIA A. HUBLEY

"Good morning, First Sequoia Bank and Trust, Jeremy Broderick speaking. How may I help you?"

"This is Jill Maynard, in the Wire Transfer Unit at bank headquarters. May I please speak to the person that handles wires at your branch?"

"You're speaking to him. I'm Jeremy Broderick, I handle all wire transfers at this San Jose branch."

"Jeremy, I hope you can help me. I have a rejected wire transfer in the amount of two hundred fifty thousand dollars for a Robert Rodriquez, and I've traced the routing number to your branch. The account number is 509998445. Could you please check and see if you have the account?"

Quickly, Jeremy input the numbers into his computer. The message returned was, *Account Not Found.* It suddenly came to him in a flash, a complete insight, the whole plan, every detail. He saw that it would work. He wondered why he hadn't thought of it before.

Jeremy stalled for time. "I'm sorry Ms. Maynard, our computers have been down off and on all morning. Response time is slow. Perhaps I should call you back."

"Yes, please call when you have the information. My direct line is (555) 767-8900. "

Jeremy handled wire transfers every day, and searching for misdirected funds was a daily occurrence. Even with modern technology, all it took was inputting just one wrong number and millions of dollars could be lost indefinitely. In his ten years with the bank, he figured he'd located well over a billion dollars. His heart pounding, the euphoria washed over him, and he felt a surge of power in his fingertips as he began to look for the lost account.

Quickly, Jeremy searched the branch database for accounts with the common name of Robert Rodriquez. Undaunted by the three hundred twenty-seven accounts in the name of Robert Rodriquez, he scrolled down the list, searching each account for the last transaction date. Narrowing the search to three inactive accounts, he chose the most dormant of the three. He was surprised that even the account number was similar to the one Jill Maynard had given him. He could pull it off. As he researched the inactive account, he was certain this Robert Rodriquez would not notice the $250,000 deposit was missing. After all, his Mr. Rodriguez hadn't touched the five million dollar balance in the account in thirteen months. His confidence building, Jeremy knew it was indeed his lucky day — thirteen was his lucky number.

"Jill, this is Jeremy Broderick from the San Jose branch, I've located the Robert Rodriquez account. The account number should be 509988446."

"Jeremy, I knew it, it's always the account number that's the problem. Advise Mr. Rodriquez it'll be in his account tomorrow morning. Thanks."

For a moment after Jeremy hung up the phone, he felt a twinge of guilt. But the moment passed, and many thoughts swirled inside his head. He could justify his actions. After all, what appreciation was he shown for ten years of hard work and loyalty to First Sequoia Bank and Trust? He certainly hadn't been compensated for his diligence, so he'd taken matters into his own hands. It had been so easy. Tomorrow morning he'd be rich! And there was no way anyone could tie it to him. The perfect crime. All he had to do was take care of one little detail first.

The little detail was a new address for Robert Rodriquez. Jeremy returned to the database and changed the address to his own. Notification of the wire transfer would go to his mailbox at his apartment.

The day couldn't end soon enough for Jeremy. His first instinct was to stop at the Jaguar dealership on the way home. His Jeep was in and out of the shop more times than he could count. His Visa statement could prove it. The old gunmetal gray Jeep sputtered as he passed the new Jaguars glistening under the lights, beckoning for him to come on in. Maybe he'd buy himself a red Jaguar for his next birthday. After all, turning thirty was supposed to be special. Instead, Jeremy headed for home, a one-bedroom apartment hidden behind a grove of birch trees on a quiet street in south San Jose.

As usual, dinner consisted of a glass of merlot, a grilled cheese sandwich and a can of tomato soup. Before Jeremy took a sip of wine, he lifted his glass and made a toast. "Tonight is the last night I'll have a poor man's dinner. Tomorrow and thereafter it'll be filet mignon!"

Unable to sleep, Jeremy tossed and turned, prioritizing what he would do at the bank the following morning. Not wanting to draw attention to himself, he knew he couldn't transfer all of the money at once into his account. It'd be five hundred dollars at a time.

For the next three months Jeremy transferred five hundred dollars every week into his checking account. He'd barely made a dent in the two hundred fifty thousand dollar windfall that had come his way.

The extra money had paid for the repair of his Jeep, a full freezer of filet mignon steaks, and season tickets to the San Jose Sharks. He tried not to draw attention to himself, knowing patience was the key to his escapade.

Then one chilly, rainy evening Jeremy sat in his Jeep snarled in commuter traffic. To ease the boredom he turned on the radio and a traffic report blared through his speakers: "The tie-up on Highway 101 due to flooding…thirty-five cars in pileup… emergency vehicles en route to scene."

Hours passed as Jeremy, with hundreds of other stranded commuters, watched emergency vehicles plow their way toward the injured. Mangled steel and flesh was strewn everywhere, the smell of burning tires and the musky odor of blood filled his nostrils. Sirens drowned out the cries for help. Distraught by the horror, none of the stranded commuters paid heed to the warning to stay in their vehicles. Jeremy paced back and forth, speaking to no one. He'd even forgotten about the first Sharks hockey game of the season.

A policeman's whistle sounded in the distance, and he motioned and yelled for them to return to their vehicles. Finally, Jeremy and the other stranded commuters were rerouted from the scene.

Once in his apartment that evening he found he'd lost his taste for filet mignon. He fixed a grilled cheese sandwich and a can of tomato soup before going to bed. Jeremy tossed and turned, awakening, reliving the mangled steel, the body bags, and the faint cries for help almost drowned out by the blaring sirens. The next morning the visions of the accident scene remained embedded in his mind. It was his thirtieth birthday, but he didn't feel like celebrating. He dialed City Hall's toll-free number.

On the second ring a gruff voice answered, "City Hall."

"This is First Sequoia Bank and Trust calling. This morning's news announced a special fund was being set up for the victims and families of last night's tragedy on Highway 101. I'd like to speak to someone about a sizable anonymous donation for the fund. We'd like to do this by wire transfer. Could you please give me the information?"

Curtly, the voice from City Hall replied, "No, I haven't heard anything about a special fund. Sorry, I can't help you."

Oblivious to the monotonous dial tone ringing in his ear, Jeremy sat dazed, his thoughts muddled, finally concluding that the phone call was the last chance to redeem himself. As he hung up the phone, he sighed, then whispered, "Maybe I'll buy the red Jaguar after all."

THE VISIT

MARTIN DODD

I first saw Nancy on September 5, 1951. We were sixteen and in high school. She stood at the front of the school auditorium that served as study hall. Her face was surrounded by an aura, and to this day I remember every detail about her appearance, from the double ellipse gold barrette in her hair to the pennies in her loafers. I sat in the fifth row, next to my best friend. "My God," I said to him, "look at that girl. I'm in love. We're gonna get married. She'll be the mother of my children." Fifteen months later our first child was born. We were together almost constantly, until her death on the forty-ninth anniversary of that day I first saw her. Nancy entered my life like lightning and left like a setting sun, leaving her warmth as evening becomes night.

Nancy means "child of grace," and she gracefully accepted challenges in life that I could see only as calamities. Throughout her illness, we received unexpected and sustaining gifts: a chance meeting, a book title, a song from the past at the right moment, and many others. I called these gifts coincidences. She would reply, "There are no coincidences."

In our last conversation, she said: "Don't waste your life mourning for me. You'll need a new girl to show off for. You've been my dragon-slayer, my knight in shining armor — my Lancelot." That night was pain and morphine, the next day morphine-fog and death. There are dragons that cannot be slain.

For three months following her death, many coincidences hinted at Nancy's continuing presence, and in one vivid dream we were tightly embracing. When I awoke, I still felt her arms around me, holding me close. For a minute or more I thought she really was there. I called that dream *the visit.* The coincidences grew further apart, and then came no more.

In the grief support groups I attended, others spoke of difficult times: birthdays, anniversaries, and holidays. Our forty-ninth wedding anniversary approached, and I fretted as to how I would spend that day. The thought came to me to retrace the last anniversary we shared preceding her illness. Perhaps I could connect to what was lost.

In early 1999, Nancy had not been feeling well. After tests, the doctor called to say, "There's a shadow on the x-ray, so I've scheduled a CT scan for April 13th." Our forty-seventh anniversary was on April 10th, an event that suddenly became very important. We decided to spend "our day" at Ventana Inn in Big Sur, south of Carmel.

We arrived about two o'clock. She slept most of the afternoon on the window seat. For perhaps two hours I looked at her, going over our life together. I thought back over past celebrations of our union: the growing, leaving, and marriages of our children and the joy of our grandchildren. Then I thought of losing her after all these years. I felt alone and scared.

When she awoke, we went to dinner. Our "table for two" was next to a window overlooking the patio. After dinner we walked outside. Then, we went to the gift shop where she bought a card on which she later wrote a message: "To My Lancelot."

Now, two years later, I drove from Salinas to Big Sur. On the way, I listened to Johnny Mathis sing *our* songs. I prayed for her to visit me as in my dream. I wanted to feel her arms around me.

I checked into the same room where we had stayed. I watched home videos of our family and us and wrote a letter to her. It all felt stilted and forced. Later, I had dinner at the same "table for two." The waiter asked if he should remove the extra place setting. I asked him to leave it, and ordered coffee for me and a glass of white wine for Nancy. I placed her glass by the plate across from me. It seemed that others were looking at the glass of wine and empty chair, maybe thinking I had been stood up.

After dinner, I picked up her glass and walked onto the patio. The night's shadows matched my mood. I renewed my plea to Nancy for a visit, whispered a toast to her, and then slowly poured the wine into the small bushes that edged the patio. I felt a little foolish for retracing our last anniversary together as if it would produce magic, but was compelled to continue, so I headed for the gift shop, as we had two years before.

As I entered, the young woman behind the counter greeted me. "Good evening. Let me know if I may I help you with anything."

I wandered around the shop, staring blankly at the shelves. I stopped at the card rack and saw a duplicate of the card Nancy had chosen on our visit.

The woman asked, "Are you here on a special occasion?"

"Yes — sort of a personal quest."

At that moment, I became aware of the soft vocal music in the background. I said, "The music is very pleasant."

"It's Loreena McKennitt. Do you know her work?"

"No." I closed my eyes, and focused on the words.

...Who is this? And what is here? / And in the lighted palace near / Died the sound of royal cheer; / And they crossed themselves for fear/ All the Knights at Camelot;/ But Lancelot mused a little space / He said, "She has a lovely face; / God in his mercy lend her grace, / The Lady of Shalott."

I must have gasped, as the woman asked, "What's the matter?"

"The words — "

"Beautiful, aren't they? It's 'The Lady of Shalott,' by Tennyson. The words are in here." She handed me the pamphlet from the CD box and continued, "I'll play it again."

I read along as I listened to the singing of the haunting poem about the Lady weaving her life, chancing a reflection of Sir Lancelot in her mirror, and then dying. In the back of the pamphlet, I found McKennitt's explanation of her work:

> *I have long considered the creative impulse to be a visit–a thing of grace, perhaps, not commanded or owned so much as awaited, prepared for. A thing, also, of mystery. This recording endeavors to explore some of that mystery. It looks as well into...influences of the Celts...With their musical influences came rituals around birth and death which treated...this life itself as a visit. Afterwards one's soul might move to another plane, or another form...*

I felt enveloped, whole—joyful. I turned to the pamphlet cover. With my eyes welling with tears, I read the title—*The Visit.*

THE RELATIONSHIP
HELEN OLSON

She carefully climbs the stepladder
Up to the out-of-reach place
Where her beautiful, treasured china awaits.

She says it's up this high so it remains safe.
Yet we know it's because she seldom brings it out.
Both of course are true.

She prizes her lovely china for its beauty,
And for the pleasure it offers
When she brings it forth.

But because it's so hard to grasp
She seldom realizes the joy
That her special treasure offers.

One day she reaches, though her arms are weak
And a delicate cup crashes to the floor.
Its death lies there reflecting back memories,
Joy that was made in its life with this woman.

And she knows this piece will be no longer,
But there are many others to enjoy.
She must place the wealth of her treasure
In a place where it is always in her sight and reach,
There to enrich her life on any day,
For many treasured times to come.

MY PAPAGENO

MAY WALDROUP

Thin, reedy flute tones reached my ear, no melody, just reedy random notes coming closer and louder with every step. My friend Papageno was coming through the Barnyard.

I looked down into the garden and there he was as if he had stepped out of Mozart's opera, *The Magic Flute*. He walked purposefully, playing his music sometimes on one, sometimes on two little colored flutes from which he would pipe two different notes into the air, announcing his approach, then fading slowly as he walked on. His steps were never hesitant; he knew where he was headed, it was his future. He had no home, he had no job, he lived in a lean-to, sometimes here, sometimes there.

I watched him as he passed, his straight back carrying an expensive green backpack. His felt hat, set at just the right angle, had a long turkey feather stuck in a leather headband pointing toward where he had come from. His gray ponytail made a human connection between hat and backpack and was a contrast to the dark green down jacket he always wore. Clean blue jeans were tucked into suede lace-up boots.

We would not meet today. I would not get a little moment to look into his bright blue eyes. I would not have a short exchange of words with him:

"How are you?"

"I am good, *da!*"

He never said yes, it was always "*da*" as though he had plucked that one word out of the Russian language. Had he, I wondered?

I knew so little about him.

117

For months I would not see him, until suddenly the reedy flute tones would come together with my Pagageno, and he would look just the same, just as well groomed, even his beard was always in neat order, always the same.

"How are you?"

"I am good, *da*!" and with "*da*" the air would become perfumed with the aroma of consumed gin. It was a powerful scent and sometimes his eyes would water. Were they tears of joy at having consumed his favorite beverage, or was it something else?

I knew so little about him.

He liked to buy incense to burn in his little lean-to. Did he burn it while he sat near the Carmel River and had his daylong cocktail hour? Did he sit and contemplate nature, rubbing the little jade stone before he had given it to me to keep as a treasure, a treasure he had rubbed smooth with his fingers, long, well-formed fingers decorated with strong long nails that nature and life would color when water and scissors would not alter them?

"How are you, Papageno?"

"I am good, *da*! I like your name for me. Where did you get that idea?"

I explained Mozart's opera to him and told him about Papageno, the bird catcher who played his flute when he walked through the forest. I did not elaborate; I didn't tell him about the dragon, about the maidens who killed the dragon, about Tamino, and so on.

He liked the bird catcher, although he said he would never hurt a bird. He assured me that he loved nature, the trees, the river, and the wildlife; he could never live in a house. He had to sleep where he was free, under the stars, to see the moon, to see the sun rising. That was his world, the world he loved.

"My mother is coming to visit me and I am going to take her to lunch at the Thunderbird on Thursday!" He added this news to our Papageno conversation.

And there he was on Thursday, standing in line at our food counter to give the order. Next to him stood an elderly woman, short, a little plump, a lady you would like to be your grandmother. She was comfortable with life, and kindness had etched its marks on her face. My kind of woman. Next to her, a gentleman, he too looked kind but did not seem to be too involved in the goings-on. The three found a table on the patio. Papageno solicitously seated his mother, pulling her chair out and pushing it close to the table for her comfort. He looked over to the gentleman and when he was seated, he too sat down and the three of them fell into conversation. There I left them, happy that Papageno had such good manners, happy that his "mom" seemed to be a kind, loving and understanding woman.

It has been a long time since I heard the sound of the flutes. Where was my Papageno? I had heard that the homeless had lost the freedom of living along the Carmel River, and in Hatton Canyon, or even behind the Barnyard. I could understand the reluctance of our citizenry to accept the homeless into our society. Few, if any, were like Papageno. Even he talked about the "others", that they were "this..." or "that..." He told me more than once that he was protecting the Barnyard from "them." I am sure he was. Even so, evidence of their nightly occupancy of hallways and protected corners was ever present.

Not long ago when the last of the century was bowing to the new, he stood in front of me in the bookstore, clean-shaven and with hair short, his stylish, expensive hat sitting well on the newly shaped haircut. His jacket and trousers, his boots and his knapsack were all of the best quality.

"Well...Papageno, you look wonderful, where are you living, what has happened since I last saw you?"

"*Da*," his eyes were still so blue and they were smiling.

"*Da*," his breath was as clean as a mountain brook.

"*Da*, I am living in a house, *da*, I am not drinking anymore, *da*, I am well!"

He said so little and yet he said it all.

So few words to describe the giant step he had made.

We held hands for a moment and then he turned to leave. I had looked again into those blue eyes and in them thought I had seen a faint longing...a longing for the days when he was free to roam, his flutes playing the music of his soul.

EPILOGUE:

Papageno is gone now, he died of pneumonia. I listen for his flute notes at night, when surely he must walk the paths of heaven.

WOMAN'S VOICE

CAROL BROWN KAUFFMANN

Sometimes she has the voice of a kitten,
tentative and small,
a dress rehearsal of things to come.

Sometimes she has the voice of a house cat,
insistent and demanding,
a sense of the power she will have.

Sometimes she has the voice of a wild cat,
quick and deep,
important matters depend on it.

Sometimes she has the voice of a lioness,
a passionate, courageous roar,
her triumphant soul emerges.

EASY MONEY

KEN JONES

"*Jesus*, Joey! Where'd you get that?" The amber streetlight glistened off the outline of the pistol as it slid back out of sight under Joey's denim jacket. "You didn't say anything about a gun."

Joey smiled and took a long pull from his cigarette. "Gives us the edge, Terrance." Terry hated it when Joey called him that. It made him feel small, and Joey knew it. Seeing the gun in Joey's waistband made him feel smaller yet, even more out of control.

Joey pulled away from the intersection. After a few blocks he turned into the Quick-Go parking lot just past Highland and parked at the far end of the building. He tossed a red knit ski mask to Terry. "Here, put this on when I tell you to." They waited for the small parking lot to empty. When the last car had driven away, Joey flicked his cigarette out the window. "Let's rock 'n roll."

Terry had to run to keep up as they hurried toward the store entrance. He squeezed the mask in a tight fist and followed along.

Joey walked straight to the cold beer case and pretended to look at labels. Terry did the same.

"Help you guys?" the young clerk called from the counter.

"Now," Joey whispered, slipping his mask over his head. Terry did the same. Again he had to hurry to keep up as Joey ran toward the counter.

"You sure can, sport," Joey yelled, holding the gun at arm's length, pointed at the man's face. Joey hopped from one foot to the other, the gun waving slightly as he danced.

The clerk jerked away from the counter, smashing into the shelves behind him. Several bottles fell to the floor. His mouth opened, but no words came.

Joey grabbed Terry by his sweatshirt and pushed him around the counter. "Get the money," he barked, still hopping and looking around the empty store in quick jerks.

Terry stared at the register and started pushing buttons. The drawer didn't open. He pushed more buttons and the register began to emit a high-pitched whine.

"Open it!" Joey shouted at the shaken clerk, bouncing closer to the counter, moving the gun to within inches of his nose. "Do it, man!" Joey commanded over the squeal of the register. The clerk quickly turned a key on the side of the register and the sound stopped. The drawer slid open and the clerk resumed his crucifix-like position against the shelving, broken glass crunching under his feet.

Terry stood as if in a trance—he felt like he was watching all this on TV. In the sudden relative silence, he heard his heart pounding fast against the top of his head and the strangely detached music playing softly from the ceiling.

"C'mon man, move it," Joey hollered, jarring Terry back into the scene.

He scooped the bills out of the drawer into a paper bag, and started to collect the change too.

"Forget that," Joey yelled, "pull the drawer out."

Terry obeyed and found a couple of fifties and an unopened roll of quarters below the drawer amid checks and other papers. Unseen by Joey, he slipped the roll of quarters into his pants pocket. "That's it," Terry said. He started toward the door.

Looking back from the doorway, he saw Joey still holding the gun to the clerk's face, making no move toward the door. "Let's go," Terry called. Joey didn't move.

"Please don't," the man whispered.

Joey stopped hopping. Terry saw a dark stain begin on the front of the clerk's pants.

"Let's go!" Terry shouted. He finally exhaled when he saw Joey start to walk backwards toward him, still holding the gun high.

Once outside, Joey turned and ran to the car. Terry had barely closed his door when Joey jammed the car in reverse and spun the wheels backing away from the building. He slammed the car into drive and screeched out of the parking lot.

They stopped beside Terry's rusty Falcon in the parking lot of the packing plant where they both worked.

Joey grabbed the bag out of Terry's lap and started to count its contents. "Man, is this all of it? *Shit.*" He counted the money again and handed Terry a wad of bills. "Here's your cut, Terrance, a hundred and sixty-three bucks." Terry took the money.

"Why're your hands shaking, Terrance? You scared? Like that big baby back there?"

"I thought you were gonna pop him."

Joey laughed.

Terry folded the money into his pocket and got out of the car.

* * *

Terry slipped the key into the lock and turned it slowly, not wanting to awaken his wife or the twins if they were asleep. He closed the door quietly and walked into the cramped front room.

His wife Barbara sat on the sofa, massaging her rounded stomach. "Hi honey," she said. "How'd it go today?"

"Same ol'," Terry said. He kissed her upturned smile and sat heavily beside her. "How're the girls?"

"Tracy almost took a step on her own today!"

"Wish I could'a seen that."

"There'll be more, trust me. As soon as one of 'em starts walking, the other'll have to. Either to chase her sister or run from her."

Terry felt the bulge of money in his pocket. Like the other times, he'd gradually slip it into the pot to help with groceries, rent, or stuff for the kids. He wanted to make it on what he earned at the plant, but there was no way.

"I talked to Mr. Smith today," Barbara said, watching the silent movement on the TV. They often watched with the sound turned down so the girls could sleep.

"What did *he* want?"

"I called *him*. He said we could have an extra week on this month's rent, but that we had to be on time next month or he'd have to think about us staying here."

"A real prince," Terry said, not hiding his contempt for their landlord.

"I could go back to work."

"Oh, right. Forget what you're carryin' there?" He put his hand gently on his wife's tummy. "Besides, day care would clean us out. And don't even start about your mother. No way the kids are gonna stay with her. We'll make it. Don't worry. End of discussion!"

Barbara rose stiffly, stretched and rubbed her back. "Want me to heat up your dinner?"

"Nah, I'm gonna take a shower and crash. Been a long week."

"Oh, I almost forgot, you got a letter from your brother today."

Terry felt his skin tighten. That's all he needed…more preaching from his perfect brother. Following Barbara's gesture, he snatched the letter from the countertop and carried it into the bedroom. He read it twice, then put it back in its envelope and stuffed it into his pocket.

He stood in the shower until the hot water and soap had completely washed away the bitter smells of raw meat from the plant and the scared sweat from his overtime with Joey. As he padded back to the bedroom, he looked down into the crib at his sleeping girls. They'd need more room pretty soon; one crib wouldn't work for long the way they were growing.

Barbara walked softly into the bedroom and peeked at the twins. She pulled their blanket up a little, then stretched out on the bed next to Terry. "Where'd these come from?" she asked, fingering the roll of quarters on the nightstand.

"Got 'em for you after work. For the washer."

"Thanks sweetie." Barbara formed herself the best she could against his side.

* * *

On Mondays, Terry worked the beef line, the hardest of all the lines. When the whistle blew for first break, he was glad for the rest...until he saw Joey walking down the line toward him. Joey's swagger made Terry think of the way John Travolta walked in the movies, except Joey didn't have the class to pull it off.

"Morning Terrance." He draped a blood-spattered sleeve around Terry's shoulder and continued to strut, pulling Terry along with him. "Got another job for Friday," he whispered. "Big one this time. Meet ya in the parking lot, same's always."

"I don't know, Joey. I think I already got somethin' goin' that night."

Joey stopped walking and pressed Terry against the wall. Terry could feel the bulletin board's pushpins dig into his back. Joey tightened his grip around Terry's neck.

"Bullshit! Same time. Don't be late." Joey removed his arm, spun around and pranced back up the line, flirting loudly with the women he passed.

Terry's hands shook so badly he spilled half of his coffee on the way from the machine to the break table. He put the cup down, rubbed his hands dry on his pant legs and took a couple of deep breaths. Steadied a little, he took a careful two-handed sip, then pulled his brother's letter out of his pocket. He read it again:

Hey Little Bro.

Hope everything's cool for you guys in Chicago. Judy and I are pretty good, and Robert's team just won their first ball game. Can you believe it? Now they can say they're one for nine! Hey, they try hard. How are the girls? Thanks for the pictures you sent, they look just like their mother, thank God.

Okay, you've heard it before, but keep reading. Here's the deal. You, Barbara and the kids got to get out of that slum you're living in and come to New Mexico. My business is really taking off, and I can't find enough good men to help me. I know what you're thinking... but it's not like that. It's <u>not</u> charity! It's an opportunity and it's here for you.

Say the word and I'll even come get you. We'll work out the move and you guys can stay with us until you get settled, don't worry about that.

Please, Terry. Think about it. Call me!

Kiss everybody for me.

Tom

It would be like admitting I was a failure, he thought. How could he explain it to Barbara? A couple more years at the plant and he'd be making some good money. Enough, he hoped.

* * *

The week passed quickly. Terry's body had somehow managed to work the conveyers, cutters and boxers, but his mind had not been on the job. When the final whistle blew on Friday, he was thankful he still had all his fingers.

He had just closed his locker when Clarence Hathaway, his line supervisor, walked up to him. "Hey Terry," Clarence said. "Got a minute?"

Terry liked the big black man with his quick smile and straight talk. "Sure, what's up?"

"It's none of my business, and you on your own time now, so you tell me to get lost if you want, okay?"

"What's on your mind, Hath?"

"I seen you hangin' with Joey a lot lately. Man, that one just plain ain't *no* good. You oughta stay away from him, you know? You gotta think of that family of yours. You got a future here, man. Don't blow it."

"Yeah, I hear ya. It's just that Joey's a hard guy to stay away from sometimes."

"I'm just sayin'." Clarence smiled. He gave Terry a slap on the back and walked away, calling back over his shoulder as he walked, "Don't be waitin' too long. That boy's headin' for some *big* trouble." Terry nodded.

He'd almost made it to the gate behind a line of other cars waiting for the light when Joey caught up with him, running. He slapped his hands on the open windowsill and stuck his head inside the car. "Where do you think you're goin'?" he said, breathing hard. Their shift had ended only minutes ago but Terry could smell beer on Joey's breath.

"I told ya, Joey. I got somethin' else on tonight."

"Like hell you do. Park this thing and let's go."

Terry gripped the wheel. "I ain't goin' tonight."

"Quit messin' around, Terrance. Park this heap and let's go!"

Terry had expected Joey to be pissed. "I ain't goin'," he said again.

Joey leaned farther into the car. He opened his jacket exposing the shiny handle of the gun. The light changed and the cars behind started to honk impatiently. Joey reached across the wheel and tapped the picture of Barbara and the twins that Terry had taped to the dash. "Cute family," Joey said with an exaggerated grin. "This is the last job you miss, Terrance. You read me?"

Terry couldn't think past the moment. He felt a rivulet of sweat run down his back and his legs felt hollow. "Yeah, yeah. I read ya."

Joey stood back with a smirk as Terry drove on.

* * *

"You're home early." Barbara dried her hands and walked sideways into his arms. "This is a treat."

"Yeah, caught all the green lights tonight. Want to order pizza?"

"Pizza? Sure, what's the occasion?"

"No occasion, just thought you'd like not to cook, that's all."

"Yeah, pizza sounds good. I'll call 'em, you go get cleaned up."

They sat at the kitchen table over the empty pizza box and soda cans. Terry looked forward to the weekend, but the thought of seeing Joey again on Monday made the pizza rise a little in his throat. He'd think about that later. Now, he needed a diversion.

"Anything on TV?"

"Let me check," Barbara said, reaching for the *TV Guide* and turning on the set.

A "Breaking News" banner splashed across the bottom of the TV screen. An old picture of Joey filled the upper right corner of the screen, the rest showed a woman holding a microphone in front of the Wal-Mart. Dozens of police cars with their lights flashing reflected in the glass doors behind her. The camera panned away from the woman to two yellow sheets covering uneven forms on the ground. He turned up the sound in time to hear the woman say: "One of the two slain robbery suspects has been identified as a local man, Joseph Arthur Harris, twenty-three, an employee of McBride Packing. Police say the two men entered the store at approximately..." Terry turned the set off.

Barbara looked up from the *TV Guide*. "Aren't we gonna to watch a movie? What's wrong? You look like you just saw a ghost."

"Nothin'." Terry went to the window, opened it and took several deep breaths. Barbara came to him and put her arms around his waist.

"What's wrong?"

That could have been me, Terry thought. *I could be dead right now.* He turned quickly away from his wife's questioning face.

"Are you cryin'? What's goin' on, Terry? Tell me."

Terry pulled away and walked into the kitchen. He pushed his hands into his pockets and felt his brother's letter. The television pictures of police and yellow sheets on the ground burned in his mind. All the strength seemed to flow out of him and he collapsed onto a chair. He spread the letter out on the kitchen table. "Tom's asked me to come work for him."

"In New Mexico?" Barbara's mouth dropped open and her hands came to her face. She sat across the table and took Terry's hands in hers.

For as long as he could remember Terry had had trouble living up to his brother's life. Tom seemed to get all the breaks while Terry took the falls. This was just the latest in a series. He looked across at his wife. "It means I've failed you. It means we couldn't make it on our own," he said softly.

"No! It means your brother loves you. I love you. You haven't failed me, or the girls, or little what's-his-name here." She patted her stomach. "If we go, it'll be your decision. You'll have made it happen. Oh, Terry...it feels like the right thing. Can we go? Please...?"

The sound of sirens passed on the street below and the image of Joey's face staring into the car alternated in Terry's mind with that of the two yellow sheets and flashing lights at the Wal-Mart.

Terry pushed his tears back inside and picked up the phone.

JUST IN CASE

Patricia Matuszewski

"You're kidding. You went to a psychic? You don't believe that stuff, do you?" I asked as I opened the gray steel door to the faculty room of Philadelphia's Anscom High School. I stood back to let my best friend and fellow teacher, Claire Kelly, go in first.

"Of course not. Not really, but you know, Letty's good. I've gone to her weekly group session twice. She's told me stuff she couldn't possibly have just guessed about."

"Like where you lost the keys to the Bug?"

"Well, you have to admit she couldn't have just guessed they dropped out of my pocket into the cat litter when I was changing it."

I laughed and nodded, "Why are you really going to her?"

"To hear from my brother. I have to find him."

"I hope you do, Claire. I know this has been eating away at you."

"Now I have a bit of hope at least. Come with me, Carol. You always like to learn about new things so you'll find it interesting. You just work, work, work. Time to do something different. Besides, it's free. We'll go to a late dinner afterwards."

"How can she do it for free?"

"She has a regular job. This is just something she does because she wants to, her volunteer work, I guess."

We dug around the dim interior of the ancient refrigerator for our lunches, then we sat at a brown plastic table in a corner made private by the air conditioner's drone.

Claire leaned towards me slightly. "Carol, ask Letty about your mother. You always complain you've known your mother all your life and you don't know her at all. Maybe you'll find out she was an attendant on the Orient Express or had a steamy love affair with a Swedish explorer."

I started to say that the distance I felt with Mother was painful, not a joke, but instead I eyed my hastily made tuna sandwich with distaste — wilted lettuce, hundreds of calories just in the mayo. *I can stand to skip a few lunches anyway.* I pushed it back in the bag and pulled out an apple. "I've got to correct first period's essays."

"Assembly first period. Remember? Correct them tomorrow night."

Ben's out of town on business until Friday. Kara won't call before Sunday. Our weekly call, just like Mother and me, and not much more substance. So much left unsaid. Is it true, you become your mother? Well, at least there's no reason to stay home. "Okay, I'll come, but just to keep you company."

"Great. Pick you up sixish then." Claire finished her cottage cheese and pineapple, pulled her skinny self up, scrunched up her lunch bag and gathered her books. "Gotta run, hit the john, and go to the office before sixth period starts. Catch you later."

"Later." I remembered the chocolate chip cookies I'd slipped into my lunch bag at the last minute because they were about to go stale. "Waste not, want not," Mother said. "Clean your plate. Remember all the starving children in India. *They* would appreciate this food." It *was* a shame to throw out perfectly good food and I *had* saved lots of calories by not eating the sandwich. Throwing it away was really about safety. It looked a bit off. I'd skip dessert tonight. Five more minutes. I relaxed and enjoyed the cookies thinking how easy it would be if I had Claire's faith in the psychic. *What would I ask her to tell me about Mother? I already know the hard working, anxious, driven mother who took excellent physical care of my brother and me. She never let us down. She never hugged us. She was quite affectionate and natural with our many cousins. I*

132

was jealous of them. Why? Help me understand my other mother, I'd say.

* * *

Letty Bish pushed up her rimless glasses, fingered her single strand of good pearls, smoothed her skirt over burgeoning hips, ran a hand in a brushing motion across the back of her sweater, and smiled vaguely at the seven of us gathered in her handsome used-only-for-company living room.

Why, she's nervous, I thought, *and so ordinary looking. Why's she doing this anyway? She's certainly not very comfortable with us.* Despite Claire's assurance that Letty Bish didn't accept payment, I wondered if this would be a teaser to get us to buy a book or sign up for expensive individual sessions later.

Letty Bish ran her tongue nervously over her lips. "I'm glad you came. I hope I can help you. We'll just start and see. I see several of you are new. You must be wondering why I do this. This may sound strange, but I feel I have been given a gift and I have a responsibility to use it to share the messages I receive with the person they are meant for."

She warned us that some sessions are more successful than others, that some people may receive messages while others do not, and that some messages are simple and easy to understand, while others are complex and confusing. "It may take some time to understand your message," she warned. "Now I'll explain a bit about what we will be doing tonight for those of you who are new to the group," she said. "I'll talk to each of you in turn. At first, I will just ask you a bit about your life and experiences. This is necessary in order to establish a connection between us, which allows messages to come through. If one does, I'll describe to you exactly what I see and hear. I can't tell you what it means, though I may be able to help you understand it by asking questions which suggest possible interpretations."

Letty Bish concentrated her attention on each one of us

in turn. Most people in the group received messages that dealt with issues currently important to them, judging from their expressions of surprise and pleasure upon hearing that they would be moving to Chicago to take the regional sales manager position, that the significant other was indeed the lifetime other, that the visa for Romania would be issued, and that all the teachers pink-slipped would be rehired by August, including Claire. *Claire must be disappointed that she didn't receive a message from her brother.*

When my turn came, I gestured toward Claire and said, "That's okay. Just skip me. I'm here as Claire's guest."

Letty Bish looked past me as if she were watching a movie and slowly shook her head. "No, I think I have a message for you. But first I need to talk to you a bit. Is that all right?"

Claire nudged me with her elbow. I turned to her with a frown and saw the plea in her eyes. *C'mon, Carol. Say yes. Get with the program. Don't be a pain and mess it up for the rest of us.*

Put on the spot, I nodded assent, none too graciously.

Letty Bish asked, "Did you live in a city with an elevated railway recently?"

"Yes, Seattle." *Lots of cities have elevated railways – Chicago, New York.*

"But you didn't grow up there did you?"

"No." *Good guess. Americans move around a lot.*

"You grew up on a farm, but you spent a great deal of time by the sea."

"Yes." *This could apply to half the people in the room. Please finish with me and move on so we can go eat.*

Instead she became very still and watched me intently. "Why are you here?"

I wasn't expecting this. I felt all eyes were on me. Flustered, embarrassed, unnerved, I stammered out what I never meant to say, "My – my mother. I want to know about my mother."

"I see a young woman with flowing dark hair walking toward you. She is holding a toddler by the hand. The child, a boy, is carrying a basket. Does this mean anything to you?"

"No."

"The woman asks that you tell your mother that everything is all right now. They are together and she is happy. Does this mean anything to you?"

I shrugged and shook my head no, torn between the truth and a first-born's desire to placate and please. I softened my "No" by adding, "I'm afraid it doesn't."

"Did you have any brothers or sisters who died?"

I shifted in my chair trying to find a more comfortable position. "No."

"Did your mother have any brothers or sisters who died?"

Claire couldn't sit still. *She's expecting some great revelation!* My stomach rumbled. *Oh, no. Why did I come?* I rushed my answer. There were only two more after me. "Not that I know of. I'm really sorry, but none of this means anything at all to me."

"Well, that is the message." Letty Bish looked at me directly. She was silent for a moment, then spoke firmly. "It is important. I think you should tell your mother."

I could feel Claire's disappointment. Despite her protestations, she at least half-believed this suburban mom-type could see the past and predict the future. I came, and left, a curious skeptic, thinking the others well meaning but naïve and feeling ill-used by having been put on the spot. At the same time, I regretted spoiling their feeling-good groupthink. *I don't even fit into a weird group like this.*

* * *

On Saturday, I made my weekly call to my mother in Washington State. As usual, we talked about the weather, gardening, the news, friends and relatives. At the end of the call, I hesitated, feeling foolish, then asked nonchalantly, "Oh, by the way, you never had any brothers or sisters who died, did you?" I had to ask. On Monday, Claire would greet me with, "Well Carol, c'mon, what did your mom say?" *Claire calls my mother "mom."*

There was a long pause, an indrawn breath, a sigh, her voice walking on eggs. "My brother James died when he was eighteen months old. Why in the world are you asking me this?"

Secrets, more secrets. If you pretend it didn't happen, it didn't. "James? You had a brother named James?"

"He was Gerald's twin."

"Gerald's twin! You never told me Gerald had a twin!" My voice rose, edged, splintery, blaming.

Mother heard the blame. "James died *years* before I was born. I never knew him. What's this all about anyway?"

"Well, last night, just for something to do, I went with a friend to hear a medium, you know, a psychic or whatever."

I described the ordinary two-story suburban house complete with white picket fence and resident golden retriever, a psychic who looked like every-housewife, the lack of special effects—no crystal balls, candles, fake fog, haunting music or dimmed lights. I said there was no charge for the session or attempt to sell anything.

I told her I'd felt left out of the group—*what's new about that?* What the medium said to me made no sense. The others present seemed amazed and excited by her comments about their past, present, or future and obviously believed her predictions would come true.

Finally, I described Letty Bish's word picture of a young woman with flowing dark hair holding a child by the hand, a child who was carrying a basket, a woman who wanted Mother to know she and the child were together and she was happy.

"Mother," I said, "I told the psychic that none of it made any sense to me." *Claire will be thrilled to hear this means something to Mother and so will the others.*

Mother said in her usual dry, flat, ironic tone, "Guess you could say that medium was warm, at least medium warm."

136

Mother's dry humor, armor to guard against feelings. I do it too. Like mother like daughter.

Mother grew serious, sadness pulling at her voice. She would be kneading a tissue in nervous fingers, constantly busy. She sounded uncomfortable and embarrassed. "You know I don't believe in that kind of stuff, never have. Still — that image, the flowing dark hair, and the being together and happy, and...especially the basket."

"What do you mean, especially the basket?"

Mother paused again and then said, "I hope she *is* with James."

"Hope *who* is with James?"

"My mother. She had such beautiful long black hair. She brushed it one hundred strokes a day. She would sit by the window in her upstairs bedroom brushing her hair, looking past the mirror. I don't think she knew I was in the room. People said she was different before James died."

"Different how?"

"Happy. I never saw her happy. She was always remote, unavailable. I don't mean physically. She was there but not there. She would go to bed for days with migraine headaches. She was a good person, kind, but not affectionate or spontaneous.

I thought, *but Mother, you are describing yourself. You took good physical care of us. You protected us kids when Father was crazy drunk. We could trust you. But we never knew you. I still don't.* "I hope she's with James too. But I can't believe you never told me you had a brother who died."

There was a clink of spoon against cup, a pause for a sip — I knew she was drinking black coffee, she always did — another sigh. "It was all so long ago. What was there to say?"

"Well, how did it make you feel?" Would this random image, gift of a stranger, help me understand why my mother was so emotionally shut down?

Mother continued, "When I was little, maybe six or seven, Gerald and I were fighting about something and he said, "You know something, Mattie bratty, if James hadn't died, you

wouldn't even be here. They only had you 'cause he died."
Her voice caught, trembled.

Tears sprung to my eyes. "You've been carrying that
around for seventy years, haven't you--thinking you were an
accident, an afterthought, alive only because someone else was
dead?"

"I'm okay. When you described the young woman with
flowing dark hair with the small child holding a basket, I thought
of my grandparents' house at Westport. It was full of baskets."

I switched the receiver to avoid telephone ear. "I
remember it too, and swimming and crabbing in the tide pools.
I loved summers by the sea. But what happened to James?"

Mother ignored this. "Grandfather Nelson's Indian
patients gave him baskets."

"Yes, yes. I remember. We used to play with them. But
what about James?"

"I'm getting to that. When my mother and father
married, they lived with Grandfather and Grandmother."

"So they were all living in the same house then?"

"Uh huh. My grandmother suffered from migraines.
The pain was so bad, Grandfather gave her morphine."

"So migraines run in the family! I didn't know that.
You and I aren't the only ones who have them." *More secrets or
left-outs, not important.*

My comment distracted her, but only for a moment.
"Anyway, one day Grandmother was so sick she left the
morphine out. That day James climbed out of his crib for the
first time and toddled into her room. The shiny blue bottle
must have fascinated him. Evidently the cap was loose. He
drank it. James was in a coma for several days before he died.
It was front-page news in the local papers. Gerald and I found
the clippings years later when we were going through her
things after Mother died.

"So the doctor couldn't save his own grandson. My God!
How awful! Your grandmother must have blamed herself the rest
of her life, too." I noticed I'd twisted the telephone cord round
and round my wrist as she talked. I shook it off, lost in thought.

"I'm sure she did. She died not long after that. She and my grandfather were both dead by the time I was born. My parents never talked to me about them or about James either. I only found out because of Gerald."

"When he told you that if James hadn't died, they wouldn't have had you?"

"I had no idea I had another brother. All the pictures had been put away."

"Did you believe Gerald?"

"No. He was always teasing me, always making up stories. But he kept saying it. Finally I asked my father. He told me that James died when he was a baby and not to say anything to my mother about James."

"So your mother didn't know you knew about James?"

"I was always afraid it would slip out."

"So you learned to be very careful of what you said."

"She seemed as fragile as the china teacups she painted with beautiful delicate flower designs. I was so afraid of making her worse, I hardly ever said anything."

That's a lesson you learned well. You've told me more today than in the whole rest of your life. "Thanks for telling me about it now. What else do you remember?"

"Years later, I was playing in the attic, I found pictures of James at the bottom of an old steamer trunk wrapped in a paisley silk shawl. One picture showed him in his coffin with a small Indian basket beside him."

"A picture of him in his coffin?"

"I don't know why. Anyway they had one."

"And he had an Indian basket in his coffin? That's very strange."

"I couldn't get it out of my mind. One day when Mother had gone out for the day, I told my father about finding the pictures and asked why there was a basket in the coffin. He made me promise never to tell Mother I found the pictures."

"That's a lot of secrets for a kid to keep."

"Too many. Anyway, he said my grandfather was a friend of Chief Ketowa of the Chehalis Indians. When James died,

Ketowa told Grandfather to put a basket in the coffin because baskets hold the soul safe as it passes from this world to the next."

I saw I was twisting the phone cord again, my version of the tissue, and instead stared at the blank television screen almost expecting it to show me her words in pictures. "So he did it. Didn't anyone object?"

"I suppose they were all too upset to care. He'd prescribed the morphine. He'd failed to save James. He had to feel guilty and helpless. He probably didn't really believe it would help, but it wouldn't hurt and it was something to do. Hedging his bets."

I nodded thoughtfully as if she could see me. "It helps to do something, anything, even if it isn't rational." I switched the receiver again. I couldn't believe what I was hearing. Suddenly, the dam had cracked and the past was seeping out.

"Carol, look, I'm really tired. I'll try to find the newspaper articles if you're interested and send them to you."

"That would be great. I'm very interested. Are you okay? You sound like you're coming out of a trance."

"That's how I feel. But I'm rather glad you asked about it all. I should have told you about it before, I guess."

"Thanks for telling me now. I know you're tired, but how about if I call mid-week and we can talk some more? Would Wednesday work?"

"Wednesday is my pinochle day. Well, after five would be okay."

"That'll be eight our time. I'll write all this down and check it with you then. Maybe we can work together to save these stories for Kara and the rest of the family."

"Maybe. We'll see. I'm pretty busy."

"I know, Mother. You've always kept busy."

"Carol, one last thing. I still have most of the baskets packed away. Will you make sure they stay in the family?"

"Of course."

"Carol — except for the tiny willow basket with the brown diamond pattern and the tight fitting top. When I die, bury it with me — just — well, just in case."

140

SHINA, FOREVER SHINA

HAROLD E. GRICE

"You Scott?"

"Yes sir." I don't break habits easily. I always "Yes sir'd Gunnys. Even as a 2nd Lieutenant I did. Especially as a field commissioned "Looie". Gunnys (Administrative Master Sergeants) run the show. They know all, see all. They keep everything in place and moving. Even to the point of getting discharged.

The Gunny held up an envelope. "It came in late," he said. "How they tracked you here to Treasure Island I'll never know. Those O.P.O. guys are something." The Gunny handed me an envelope. "I didn't know you was a lieutenant."

"I'm not. I'm a civilian."

The envelope was square and larger than normal. It had the elegant silky texture of quality paper. I read the address:

Lt. Steven E. Scott
3rd Marines,
Camp Bennet
Kamakura, Japan

I recognized the delicate handwriting. Heartache filled my chest. Memories shocked my mind. I shook myself, stuffed the envelope into my pocket.

"You all right? You look like you saw a ghost." The Gunny was looking at me hard.

I stood for a moment, then said, "No. I left them all behind. See you, Gunny." I went down to the slip.

Boarded the ferry that would take me to San Francisco. I wended my way through the end-of-day going-home crowd to the bow. Looked at the sun sinking in the fogbank that defines Frisco.

The official emblem of Japan is the rising sun, but after watching the sun go down over the West Pacific so many times on the way back, I think the opposite. To me Japan is where the sun and memories sink into the sea. The sun sets over Japan, over Shina-san. Over my Shina. The ferry pulled away from the dock. A gentle pulse pushed us toward the S.F. Ferry building.

I pulled out the envelope. Examined it. I didn't want to imagine what it would say. I might dream it would say "Meet me at the airport." But I knew it wouldn't.

I opened it. The printed message was in Japanese. It was an announcement. I couldn't read it all but I recognized the word *Kekkonshiki*, or wedding ceremony. Shina and I had discussed *Kekkonshiki* many times.

I recognized the names, Shina Hashimoto and Yokiyo Yamasaki. The insert was an announcement, the announcement of Shina's marriage. So it happens. In the empty space was a written message. The written message was in Shina's delicate hand. The lines, so even and graceful.

Grateful you being you
For letting me have honor
I love you always

Again my heart filled my chest. I had to look away. Through blurry eyes I could see Shina, hear her. I could almost feel her.

Shina.

It seemed so long ago…

Japan.

I was in Yokosuka.

I was at the park.

I sat feeding the funny-looking ducks.

The person next to me was also feeding the ducks.

142

The ducks were a dark, moldy-looking lot.
The ducks squabbled over every offering.
The ducks pushed, shoved, made a squawking racket.
Next to me was a girl.
A Japanese girl.
She wore the traditional kimono.
Dark silk kimono with scarlet slashes. ·
There was the big bow on the back.
Her hair was in the typical bun.
I could see her face, more gold than brown.
I could also see a strong chin.
Cheeks dimpled beside a straight nose.
Laughing, soft brown eyes.
She was thinner than most Japanese girls.
Slender that is, not skinny.
An older lady was in attendance.
Dressed traditionally, with her face whitened with powder.
The older lady was providing small pieces of bread from within her sleeve.
The girl's hands, casting the bread, were slender, long-fingered, elegant.

So far in my wanderings about the country, I had observed many such Japanese. The kimono with the big bow. The stilted shoes. The deep sleeves where everything was kept. The bun at the back of the head. The older more traditional Japanese women powdered their faces. I had tried to talk with them. I had even started taking language at the base. But they all seemed shy of me.

Just for the hell of it I said, "You like to feed ducks?" She couldn't possibly know English. I added, "These are especially hungry, ugly, noisy fuckers."

She giggled. "I don't think that is a proper term for these ducks. These are Peking Imperials."

I fell off the bench. "Whoops." My face must have been beet red. "I apologize. I didn't think you would understand."

"I learn American at school," she said.

"I am sorry. I didn't think anyone would be listening."

"I listen. How else would I learn?" She looked at me.

I said, "Maybe I could teach you. Or you could teach me Japanese."

"Could do such a thing?" Her voice softened, a question.

"Why not?" I looked into soft almond eyes.

"O.K. I here tomorrow," she said in a determined voice. "We start this teach."

All I could do is look up. She gave me a bow. The kind of bow you don't answer. She walked off in that quick way that girls in kimonos do that have to walk with those wooden shoes.

It is very fast.

The girl was taller than her companion.

Her companion followed.

A quick glance over the shoulder was all I got.

She was pretty?

She was nice?

It didn't matter.

It was most entertaining.

Nothing will happen.

Will I be here tomorrow?

You damn betcha.

I was out of Korea on R&R - Rest and Relaxation. Korea had taken a bad turn. About the time we Marines had gotten to Chosin Reservoir, the Chinese had jumped in. We had to fight our way out of Chosin to the coast. My company had got shot up bad. I was the last one left standing. I commanded the company for a while. We got replacements. Recruits, not officers. The company needed an officer. They made me a lieutenant. We beat the Chinese off our back to Hungnam, a seaport on the west coast of Korea. The Navy got us off the beach. They hadn't decided what to with us yet so they sent us to Japan for R&R. So I was on R&R without much to do.

I didn't find whores and drinking really to my liking. Also, now that I was a lieutenant, I had to act more respectful. So I was kind of wandering around Japan soaking up the culture as best I could.

144

It had been seven years since the Pacific part of World War II had ended with the surrender of Japan. While much of the society had been influenced by American occupation and the desire to get as much money from the Americans as possible, much of Japan remained culturally pure. Even so, this was my first opportunity to get to know a "real" Japanese.

So I returned. I was there. I had even brought some bread to feed the ducks. The ducks were not there to be fed. But I threw the bread out anyway. Suddenly a bunch of pigeons descended on the bread. The flutter of wings and the confusion of birds entertained me. I marveled at their iridescent colors and the apparent pecking order of birds.

"They beautiful, are they not?" The soft voice of the girl.

My head whipped around. "I didn't think you would come," I said.

She looked me in the eye. Her soft brown almond-shaped eyes also had a determined expression. The look said, "I do what I will."

"Well," I said, "my name is Steven. I'm from California. I am here on R&R. How about you?"

"My name is Shina Hashimoto. I am student. I am upper level—how you say—not little school person—university. I live in city long time."

"Student, city dweller. Whatever." I said the first things came to my mind. She was very nice. "What do you mean not a country person?"

"I live here all my life." She waved her hand to include the whole of the town. "I want know all things. Those they don't show. You teach me English?"

"Yes. Yes." I was going to learn of the Japanese.

So we met.

And we talked.

And we walked.

And we talked.

And we learned.

And we talked.

As I had never talked before.

145

We were seeing each other but always with her companion, her *Oba san*, her "Aunty", in attendance. We ate fish candy; we ate rice balls with seaweed.

We were passing a place on the street. It had a sign over the door. There was character writing on the sign. The sign had what looked like a bowl with steam rising. I had not yet learned to read signs. Shina looked at me with dancing eyes. "I think we eat here." We went in. The proprietor, I think he was the proprietor, a little gray man with an apron stained from many uses, bowed low: *"Hashimoto Shina san, anataga watashitachi no tokoroni kite itadaki koeni omoimasu."* ("Welcome Hashimoto Shina. We are honored that you would come into our establishment.*)*

He guided us to a table at the front window. *"Kokoni suwatte kidasai."* ("Sit here please.")

His head was completely bald except for a fringe of silver hair around the back. The room was narrow and deep. It was dark and I couldn't see much. The floor was sweep-shined. The table was rough hewn with heavy legs and a sturdy top. Smoothed from many cleanings.

There was a scattering of other patrons. All noise and eating had stopped when we entered. Slowly they began eating and talking again. Shina covered her mouth and giggled. With laughing eyes she said, the words muffled, "They talk about you. They want know you my American Marine."

The man came back and he and Shina talked rapidly. Then he disappeared into the dark at the back of the room.

"What was that all about?" I asked.

"We to have workman's lunch," answered Shina. "This is very typical Japanese restaurant."

I looked out the window. The street looked picture book village. Worn wood sidewalks on both sides of the narrow street. The street looked to be cobbles, worn dark and shiny. The storefronts across were all of wood and glass. Weathered to a soft brown. Painting wood seemed a low priority.

I watched some of the patrons. The Japanese eat rice by throwing it into their mouths. I had pretty much mastered that.

Shortly the bald man came with a tray. He set a steaming bowl of soup and a bowl heaped with rice before each of us.

I sat up straight. I looked at the soup. It was full of vegetables and things I couldn't identify. The room was suddenly silent again.

"Shina, what's going on?"

Shina put her hand over her giggle. "They waiting to see you eat. They very curious."

"I can manage the rice okay. But how do you eat soup with chopsticks?"

She giggled again. "First pick out all the vegetables, then drink the rest." She looked at me with raised eyebrow. "I get you a spoon."

"That would probably save us a lot of embarrassment."

As if reading our mind, the bald man appeared and laid a large spoon on the table.

In this manner we spent our days together.

We went to lunch, and to dinner. We had sushi, a vegetable soup with everything in it, even octopus. I learned to eat with chopsticks, to like tea. I taught the restaurant how to make hamburgers. It was near impossible as they had very little meat.

One evening Shina said, "We staying home."

Home was her house. Shina and her mother were busy in the kitchen. They fixed things they put in little dishes then put lids on. After they had done all this and put them in a basket, Shina led me down to a little house in the back behind the main house.

"We call this Tea House of Apple Blossom. We think it nice to name things." Shina rolled back screens along the walls. From covered closets she took padded pillows and spread them on the floor. Then she dragged over a stiff-legged coffee table.

Aunty-san served us. It was an interesting meal. Rice, fish cakes, noodles in soup and a light rice bread toasted over a hibachi. Shina rested on her knees in the traditional style. I sat on some pillows.

147

Aunty-san was always nearby. She could be fun. We had fun times.

We went to the Ginza and bought foolish things. A street photographer took our picture. I bought one. It was of a beautiful Japanese girl and a Marine.

As we walked, Shina pointed things out and explained. I nodded and made comments, silly if I could. Then we went on, laughing, talking and having fun. Holding hands sometimes.

We walked through the apple blossoms.

We kissed under the Great Fig Tree.

Shina's lips were soft and giving.

They tasted sweet.

I lost myself in her kiss.

Aunty-san looked away.

We walked in the country to see a man with a cow. This man, a peasant, kept the beast inside in a small stall. The man massaged the cow every day. In Japan the beefsteak was so tender it could be cut with a fork. It was also very mild. It was also very expensive.

We went to the Obon in Osaka.

We stood outside a large store window.

We studied ourselves in the reflection.

A straight, slender Japanese girl in kimono.

A tall, straight, slender Marine in uniform.

An older, very proper Japanese adult in the background.

We turned away without comment.

Shina's hand rested lightly on my sleeve.

We switched to holding hands.

"Rather nice looking couple, wouldn't you say?" I asked.

"Very nice looking couple. I think they very lucky," Shina answered.

I ducked and we kissed quickly and laughed.

Aunty-san shook her head and clucked her tongue. "*A mano jaku*" ("Silly children.")

We had an outing to the beach. Being from California, I

took some swimming trunks. Aunty-san brought a basket of lunch. At last, I thought, I would get to see the figure beneath the kimono. The figure I had held. The body I had felt through the wraps of cloth. The figure that made me sigh in my dreams.

The beach was on the ocean side of the peninsula, toward Kamakura, a long white sandy beach with these little cabins on wheels. For privacy while changing.

"You go to that one," Shina pointed. "We use this one."

We entered the little rooms on wheels. I quickly put on my trunks, gathered up my towel and stuff and went down to the sand. The sand was warm and clean. The air was warm and soft. The waves were small but made a nice pop as they broke. Not at all like a crowded California beach with the crashing waves, but still a pleasant place. There were others on the beach. Not many.

There was ample room to be relatively private. They seemed to prefer to have distance.

I heard the door of Shina's room open. I turned and was astonished. I had thought a swimming suit, something revealing. Something very "California". What I saw was a very statuesque girl with loose black silky hair in a white cotton top and black cotton trousers. As she walked toward me, I had to admit Shina looked every bit as alluring as if she was wearing a revealing two-piece California bikini. I had to laugh.

"What so funny?" Shina wasn't too sure whether to join my laugh or not.

"Nothing. Yes. I was anticipating seeing you in a bathing suit. Not fully dressed. Something revealing."

"You man." She pushed me down into the sand.

I helped Aunty-san put up the umbrella. Aunty-san spread a large robe beneath it and sat in the shade. Aunty-san's beachwear was a less formal cotton-looking kimono. It was a pale color. I was surprised, as I had never supposed her to wear anything but dark.

Shina and Aunty-san were chattering away about the others on the beach.

"Lets go for a swim," I challenged. I was ignored. I went to the surf. The water was warm by California standards.

149

I went in, dove through a wave. Came up beyond the surf. Swam around a little, dove to the bottom, looked at the sand. There were no sand dollars.

I hollered and waved for Shina to come in. She didn't move. They stayed on the robe, talking. I caught a wave and body-surfed in as far as it would take me. Scooped up a double handful of seawater. Walked up to them. They were still talking. I let some of the water dribble on Shina's head. They stopped talking. I dumped what water was left.

I didn't think this slight girl, who was always restricted in a kimono, could move so fast. On her feet in a flash. I took off for the water. Hit it full speed, stretched out through a wave. Beyond the surf, I stood chest deep in the water, laughing as I turned around. Shina wasn't in sight. Nowhere to be seen. Suddenly, my legs went out from under me.

I came up gasping.

Shina was there.

Laughing at me.

I went after her.

Shina could swim like a fish,

Even in those clothes.

I couldn't catch her.

We went around and under.

I would dive to get to her.

When I got there she would be somewhere else.

Finally, Shina was in the waves.

I dove and let the undertow take me out.

I came up in front of her.

I had caught her, or she let me catch her.

I hugged her.

I studied the light golden olive skin.

Her shiny soft brown almond eyes.

Silky black hair washed over her face.

Beneath the thin, wet cotton was the soft feel of a girl.

Beneath the softness was the feel of live strength.

We kissed as the surf broke over us.

Aunty-san blew a whistle.

150

Like a schoolyard whistle.
We looked at Aunty-san.
We looked at each other.
We started laughing.
Aunty-san had a whistle!
A wave knocked us over.
We rolled in the surf. We got up sputtering and laughing. Ran hand in hand up to the towels and flopped down. Shina lay on her back. We were still laughing and giggling. Aunty-san and her whistle.

I rose to my elbow. There before me was this dream of a girl. I could hardly take my eyes off the form revealed through the wet cotton. She glowed. The wet cloth clinging to each curve and contour. Her breasts rising and lowering with each breath. Her flat body rippling with each giggle. Shina so immediately affected me I had to lie on my stomach.

Aunty-san draped a towel over her saying, "*Shina-san, kaze o hikanai yo taoru o kakete agemasho.*" (Shina-san, let me cover you, you will chill lying wet like that.)

I looked into Shina's face.
Her eyes were looking intently into mine.
I lost myself there.
I lifted some of the soft, silky tendrils from her brow.
What started as a swift kiss turned into more.
It became a "*There is no one else in the world, just you and I*" kiss.
With just our lips touching.
We became a part of each other.
I felt the light touch of her hand.
It rested softly on the back of my neck.
The kiss was gentle and tasted like salt.
The intensity became magnetic.
A complete giving of ourselves.
I became aware of a persistent pushing on my shoulder.
I looked up.
Aunty-san was holding out a bowl. "Steve-san, *ohira gohon desuo.*" ("Time to have lunch.")

It took moments to reorient. Then we sat up and had lunch of rice and some other things. I kept my towel across my lap to hide my discomfort.

The rest of the day was pleasant. Going back on the bus was more of an adventure because our things were not packed as well and stuff was always falling out. Plus we laughed a lot and looked at each other with a new intensity.

That night in quarters my dreams were filled with alluring black-haired, giggling, dimpled mermaids. They could out-swim me and catch me in the water, but I could not catch them. My limbs were so cumbersome as to barely move. The mermaids were always just out of reach. They were so beautiful. They made my heart ache. They were so stimulating that I woke in a sweat. I took a cold shower.

The days that followed were full of wonder. We talked of everything under the sun. From jobs to education. About families and houses. About where it would be nice to live.

We went to the national museum. The history of Japan was neatly displayed. It was very ornate. The displays did not include anything about the war. I wondered if it had not been long enough ago to be truthful, but did not remark on it.

We went to a flower show where all the displays were stark and very Japanese. Not the vases full of flowers I was used to. Some entries were just one or two stalks in a large vase. I asked if maybe they couldn't afford any more flowers? One display had everything upside down, two flowers in the water with the stalks up. Pretty strange.

I wondered to Shina, "Is that the way they grow them, upside down? Maybe they are from the other side of the world and that is just natural?" Shina would go, "Shh, shh, shh." Then look at me with laughing eyes.

We went to a play where the female actor was a male. Shina talked our way to backstage to meet the female lead. It was a man. God! Before she turned back into a man I thought she was beautiful.

Shina was beautiful.

We kissed as often as possible.

152

We held each other as often as possible.

We spent as much time together as possible.

We loved the same things.

Summer turned into fall. My weekends were spent with Shina. We went to the fishing port where the rocks are bound together. They are forever companions. We walked the fish market sheds. The fish were laid out in rows for buyers to choose. There were other sea things, clams, small fish, octopus and things I could not identify. The fishermen, a hard and dangerous-looking lot, bowed deeply to Shina. Respecting her bearing and charm. Aunty-san bought things.

It became rumored that the Third Marines' stay in Japan was nearing an end. We would be shipped out to the States. I was in a quandary. I had never found anyone I cared for more. Would it be proper for me to propose? I couldn't decide what to do.

The late part of the day turned warm.

Shina invited me to have tea.

We would be in the teahouse.

We entered.

We sat across from each other.

I was in uniform.

Shina wore a kimono.

A kimono of soft silk.

It was a mellow color with crossing red-brown stripes.

It pulled tight across her breasts.

It had a simple tie at the waist.

She wore her hair in a single braid.

Shina served tea in the traditional way.

Sitting on her knees.

Bending from the waist to gather and serve.

Each movement revealing the figure against the
soft cloth.

She was so graceful and elegant.

Each motion of her slender body was but a gentle
flow, a symphony of motion.

She was so beautiful I had difficulty seeing anything
else.

153

It grew dusky.
Aunty-san closed the screens.
I could hear her screw in the stops.
Shina lit a small lamp.
It gave a soft, steady, but wavering light.
Shina stood.
I started to stand.
Shina motioned me to remain seated.
She stood across from me.
Shina undid the simple tie.
She let the kimono fall from her shoulders.
It draped on her wrists.
I couldn't move.
Her rising breasts.
The arch of her neck and chin.
The swell of her hips.
Her womanhood.
Her straight long legs.
She stood tall above me.
"I think you are the most beautiful thing in the world."
"Will you have me?"
"I love you."
"Will you have me?"
"You are everything I ever want."
"Will you have me?"
 "God knows I want you."
"Will you have me?"
"Yes. No. Not like this. We have to be married."
I stood.
I kissed her lips.
Her eyes were closed.
I kissed her neck.
I kissed her breasts.
I inhaled the scent of Shina.
If I let myself go I would have her.
We would never be the same.
I would never be the same.

I let myself out through the door.
I grasped Aunty-san.
Pushed her through the door.
Aunty-san looked at me.
At my hardness.
My uniform was still in place.
She smiled and nodded.
My God!
I could have had her.
I am so stupid.
Nothing explains love like love.
Love is unexplainable.

I must talk to her father, so I made an appointment. I went to the house. The house had stucco sides but the insides were all bamboo with windows everywhere. The interior had walls but much of the inside space was divided with rolling tissue paper panels. With the panels open the garden could be seen from every room.

In apple blossom time this garden had rained soft petals of pink.

We'd skipped through them.
One skip, two skips.
Raising a storm of cloudy pink.
Aunty-san joined in.
We made a blizzard.
They laughed, a merry tinkle.
At night the panels slid here and there.
The panels closed everything off.
Even the room to Shina.
I was young and lustful.
Shina is so beautiful.
I love her so much.

I left my shoes at the threshold. Put on the little slippers they use, an idea I had come to like. I wore all my medals and ribbons. Shina was so proud of me and straightened my tie, adjusted the medals. We had a quick kiss on the lips. Aunty-san brushed the sides of my jacket, tugged the blouse to make the bars stand out.

I entered to see her father, Tsuyoshi Hashimoto. I walked in, bowed, I sat. In sensitivity to me there were pillows about. In respect to Mr. Hashimoto, I sat in Japanese style with legs crossed. I bowed, with my respect. Mr. Hashimoto returned my bow. I waited. Mr. Hashimoto was very wise. He spoke:

"You have been seeing my daughter for some time now.
I do not question your fondness for each other, my
daughter and you.
I know you are deeply committed to her happiness.
You have shown it in many ways.
I know that you are prepared to ask for her in marriage.
It is because you are honorable that this is difficult.
There are things to consider were I to approve.
Were you to marry it would be difficult.
It is likely that your love would last beyond the
anguish of ridicule.
Beyond the question of your children, and beyond
their future.
But there would be many difficulties.
There would be many personal and official difficulties.
You and your children would not be accepted by many.
Either in the American or Japanese communities.
Your children would also suffer much anguish.
Throughout your and their lives there would be
little acceptance.
I have seen it. It is so.
I do not wish my only daughter to suffer that plight.
To have that anguish.
We have had too much anguish.
Her uncle became a pilot, *kamikaze*.
He sacrificed himself on the deck of the *Yorktown*.
For no purpose in the end.
It was already too late.

My people did many unreasonable things to
many and to ourselves.
It must stop.
We are Japanese.
Five thousand years we have been Japanese.
My daughter will always be Japanese.
You are American.
Only two hundred years, you have been American.
Yet you will always be American.
We cannot meet in this day.
Later maybe, not today.
There is still too much anguish.

"In respect for my daughter and traditional Japanese manner, and in the interest of my daughter and family tradition, we have made arrangement for my daughter to be wed six months from now to the son of Mr. Yamasaki. His son will be finishing his required National Guard duties and returning home to take his position in the bank next month.

They will need uninterrupted time to become acquainted. Under other circumstances I think you would like and approve of him."

I started to protest.

Mr. Hashimoto raised his hand, palm out. I was stilled. He is Shina's father.

"There will be, of course, the presence of hurt and sadness. But should this action prevent a life of anguish, then I will have performed my duty."

My breath came in short spurts. My heart hammered at my throat. My throat hurt.

"Your Third Marines will be leaving for your homeland shortly." Mr. Hashimoto took a deep breath. He looked into my eyes intently. He said, "As a father to a man, a man of honor, I ask that you stop seeing my daughter."

Mr. Hashimoto bowed.

There was no question.

I bowed.

I rose on weak knees.

I left.
Shina and I walked out to the harbor.
I held Shina's hand.
Shina gripped my hand hard.
Her hand was not still.
She had heard.
We stopped at the edge of the quay.
Aunty-san placed a hand softly on my sleeve.
There were tear lines.
Trails through the powder on her checks.
Aunty-san bowed deeply.
Aunty-san shuffled away bowing.
Shina and I stood.
We faced each other.
Shina always wore the kimono.
She wore toed socks, wooden shoes.
She let her hair down only in the privacy of her home.
If I were a man I would steal her away.
To hell with all others.
We would have our way.
I am not that sort of man.
Her father is right.
I know that.
I am not that man.
I could not make her suffer scorn.
I loved her too much.
I examined the soft skin.
I saw the silken face I loved.
The soft brown almond eyes.
Eyes where I had lost myself many times.
I saw the Ginza, the Obon.
I could see the girl on the beach.
I could see the glowing eyes of laughter.
I inhaled the memories of Shina:
of the soft warm skin beneath the kimono;
of the awakening awareness on the beach;
of the beautiful woman in the teahouse.

My heart ached with these memories.
What we had become we could not be.
Go home!
If you love her, go home!
I touched the beautiful face.
I kissed her soft brown eyes.
I kissed the straight nose.
I kissed the welcome lips.
Then we kissed intensely.
Her arms trembled around my neck.
We looked deep into each other's soul.
Tears ran from Shina's eyes.
"I love you always."
"Shina, I will love you forever, Shina."
Her hand trembled soft upon my cheek.
It is still there.
I loved her too much.
Go home.

The rhythm of the ferry changed. I came back to what I held. The card opened. There I recognized Shina's delicate hand. Heartache filled my chest. Through blurry eyes I could see Shina, hear her reading the lines to me:

Grateful you being you
For letting me have honor
I love you always

The ferry blasted its arrival. The city skyline was before me. My eyes rose to the sun dipped in fog.
I said to the wind, "Shina, forever Shina."
I thought of the haiku I had composed. I had repeated it many times as I looked over the fantail. Looked at the sun setting over Japan. Setting over Shina.

We love, we are one
Love is unexplainable
Shina, forever Shina

The ferry bumped into the slip, pressed snug to the gangway. The crowd surged off. I followed along. They had said if I shipped over I could go to OCS, Officer's Candidate School. I could keep the bar. I had to remind them that the minimum age for OCS is twenty-one. I wouldn't be twenty-one for another three months. I declined. They reduced me to grade and discharged me.

A taxi slid up to the curb. "Need a cab?"

"Sure."

"Where to?"

"Home. Take me to the railroad. The SP Terminal."

I dumped the sea bag in the back seat, climbed in up front.

"I want to see the city," I tell him, but all I can see is Shina. The driver is yammering.

But all I can hear is Shina:

Grateful you being you
For letting me have honor
I love you always

I loved her too much.

We love, we are one
Love is unexplainable
Shina, forever Shina.

"I am going home," I said

OAK CREEK CANYON: WINTER
LYNDA SPERRY JARDINE

Silver gray day
Air silent as stone
December's advance bites
At withering leaves
Forsaken by passing
Of Fall's languid days.
Slumbering forest
Barren in repose.

Aching soul
Escapes to solitude
Embraces hungrily
Quiescent beauty
Soothed by winter's lullaby:
Cold stream, chattering pebbles
Ice claims hidden places
Warm breath rises in cold mist.

THE COLLECTOR
MARTIN DODD

The Ancient searches
place to place,
alone, unknown,
seeing and unseen.
In time, He bends,
retrieves a string
left lying
by circumstance.
From His bosom
He takes a wrapping ball
and winds this new treasure
around the rest.
Cord, or twine, or thread,
He adds them all,
and treats each length
with respect afforded best,
yet seems not to care
if it served well or poorly.

His fine collection
is molded like the sun,
a star that marks
 the cycle of our days;
a sphere when circled
returns to where begun.
When new, each thread
is pulled from its source,
cord cut,
and set to use,
until its role
is met or missed.
Then, untied,
broken, or frayed,
it is cast aside,
useless,
until redeemed
for Collector's purpose.

THE BACKPACKER

PETER HOSS

It is Christmas Eve, growing dusk, cold and chilly, at a nondescript truck stop with a mini mart, the kind that is everywhere. This one is located four miles north of Paso Robles, California, just off Highway 10l. A figure emerges from behind the mini mart, a young man looking to be in his late twenties or early thirties, with a backpack on his back with a rolled-up sleeping bag lashed to it. He has dark hair and sharp features. He looks clean cut and does not have the look of a scruffy derelict. He walks out to the road and starts walking slowly toward Highway 101. He is not thumbing a ride and gives no indication that he needs help. He is just minding his business walking down the road. Other cars pass. No one seems to take notice of him.

The backpacker trudges on to an unknown destination not knowing that, in a fleeting moment, he will make a lasting impression on the driver of one of the vehicles which does not stop, who catches only a passing glance of the backpacker and never will see him again.

The driver is a white male in his late sixties, driving an SUV loaded with Christmas gifts for grandchildren and a son and daughter-in-law, anticipating a bibulous Christmas dinner full of fellowship. This will be the second Christmas without his wife of forty years, who died suddenly eighteen months ago. The first such Christmas was a blur. The driver was born in the Great Depression, matured in the fabulous fifties, avoided serving in World War II, the Korean War or Vietnam, a veteran of peacetime

163

non-threatening military service. He became a Christian at age thirty-seven.

He is retired, in good health, financially secure, and free to do whatever he wants whenever he wants to do it. He is feeling mellow about his life.

After catching a glance of the backpacker and making eye contact for only a few seconds, the SUV driver wonders: Is the backpacker homeless? If so, how did he reach that state? What is the backpacker's destination? Does he have one? Is he destitute? The backpacker is a symbol of loneliness at a time when most people are with friends and family, but none of the drivers stop to find out about him. Where is he going? How will he spend Christmas?

Christmas music plays on the radio in the warm comfortable interior of the SUV. Thoughts in the mind of the driver of the SUV turn to the historical figure whose birthday will be observed and celebrated tomorrow, even by many who do not profess to be His followers or to accept who He said He was. His birthday seems to motivate people to be more charitable, and to extend a helping hand toward those less fortunate, even if only for a brief time. During the three years of an itinerant ministry, when His most significant teachings were reported, He was homeless and so poor that He owned only the clothes on His back when put to death. However, although homeless, He was frequently invited into the homes of people, some wealthy, as a guest, and wined and dined and treated to foot washing. He was never alone, except when He wanted to be. At all other times He was accompanied by twelve followers, faithful in part when He lived, and later, after some wake-up calls, after His death. Many holy men of other faiths have also been homeless wanderers.

The SUV driver drives on and comforts himself with the thought that he has done his service for the poor and unfortunate by taking Christmas dinners to farm workers in a labor camp yesterday. He feels a twinge of guilt that he did not stop, but reasons to himself that the backpacker was not asking for anything or giving any sign of being in distress. Besides, picking up hitchhikers can be dangerous. He knows horror stories.

He arrives at a Christmas Eve party, eats and drinks copiously, and enjoys love and fellowship. The next day he spends with his son, daughter-in-law and grandchildren in a home full of toys. The young boys enjoy their new toys and occasionally fight over them, as boys will do. Thousands spend their day in a similar fashion. Too soon the holiday is over and the driver heads home, this time with a mostly empty SUV and happy memories, feeling warm and fuzzy.

While driving home the SUV driver again sees a vision of the solitary backpacker, which keeps flashing in front of him. He returns to the truck stop where he saw the backpacker to see if he is still there. He is not. He even asks in the mini mart and restaurant behind it if anyone knows anything about the backpacker. The restaurant has a sign on the door saying that no checks or credit cards will be accepted, only cash. No one knows anything about the backpacker. The driver wonders if the backpacker had any money to buy a meal on Christmas. He realizes that he is not likely ever to know who the backpacker is, where he was going, how he spent Christmas Eve and Christmas Day, or what happened to him. Nevertheless the backpacker continues to evoke an image to the SUV driver that will recur. The driver reflects that he will never find himself in the situation in which he saw the backpacker, even though he is and will remain a recreational backpacker himself. He has never spent a Christmas without family and loved ones, and does not expect ever to do so.

The vision of the backpacker continues to reappear at irregular times with perfect clarity to the SUV driver, long after he has forgotten any other details of the

Christmas visit, what gifts he gave, what he ate for Christmas dinner.

On the days in which the vision of the solitary backpacker does not appear, the SUV driver wakes up, confident that he has led a good life, paid his dues, and deserves the good life he is leading. He passes by panhandlers and either looks past them or says, "Sorry not today, maybe later." He thinks to himself that they will just spend what he gives them on booze and drugs. When his friend asks him to substitute as a driver for Meals on Wheels, he tells him he is busy and cannot miss his golf game. "Sorry, not today but maybe tomorrow." When the requests for charitable contributions arrive in the mail, as they do almost every day, he sticks them in a file to look at, maybe tomorrow.

On the days when the vision of the backpacker reappears, the SUV driver drops small change into the hand of the panhandler and says "God bless." When his friend asks him to drive for Meals on Wheels he says, "I will be glad to, I can play golf tomorrow." Sometimes he reaches into his file, looks at a request for a charitable donation, and writes a check.

The SUV driver frequently sees homeless people on the streets of his own community, trundling their possessions around in shopping carts and rummaging through dumpsters. Often he sees them repeatedly, because they frequent the same locations. None of them has ever asked him for assistance. He has never volunteered assistance. He believes he would not know what to do or say to them directly. He occasionally donates food or money to a local homeless shelter.

The SUV driver has heard from some who claim to be experts that the homeless do not wish to change their lifestyle. He has also heard that many of the homeless are mentally ill or semi permanently stoned on booze or drugs. He has a hard time believing that anyone would want to live as the homeless live, but he has no experience on which he can draw to form a conclusion, no common ground. The gap between where he is and where the homeless are is too great to be bridged. Nevertheless, he is troubled by the existence of a homeless class in the wealthiest nation in the world. It does not seem right to him, but he does not know what to do about it.

Several times since Christmas the SUV driver has passed by the truck stop four miles north of Paso Robles. Each time he does, a mysterious force compels him to drive in and look for the backpacker he knows he will not find. If ever he were to see the solitary backpacker again, he would not know what to do or say. He might well pass him by again.

HOW TO SUCCEED
BY REALLY TRYING:
A New York Love Story

WALTER E. GOURLAY

Some people are born popular, some people achieve popularity, and some people have it thrust upon them. This is the story of how two lonely young people from the same small town came to the big city and found all their hearts' desires.

Their names were Homer T. Flack and Gretchen Himmelheimer. They both lived in Missing Gap, Iowa (population 7612 if you count the drunks in the county jail).

Homer was the most colorless boy in Missing Gap. Gretchen was the most lackluster girl. Each of them was so unobtrusive that it was two years before anyone in Missing Gap missed either of them, and nobody remembered what they looked like.

Homer traveled by Greyhound Bus. Gretchen traveled by train. Homer didn't know that Gretchen existed. Gretchen didn't know that Homer existed. Each one looked forward to all the fascinating people they would meet in New York.

Dear reader, do you remember the first day, when, with widened eyes and palpitating heart, you set foot on the fascinating sidewalks of New York? Do you remember the excitement, your dreams? Do you remember your first intoxicating glimpse of the crowds, of the traffic, of the Times Square Shuttle?

Try to imagine, if you can, arriving in New York from a place like Missing Gap, Iowa.   Try to envision Homer T. Flack setting down his big black suitcase, tied with cord from the Missing Gap General Store, on the floor of the 34th Street Greyhound Terminal, and finding romance at Nedick's hot dog stand.   Try to picture Gretchen Himmelheimer being helped by a handsome young stranger with a cleft in his chin who carried her two suitcases across Penn Station and invited her to dinner. You can't?   Well, you're right.   All Homer got from Nedick's was a hot dog and orange juice.   And nobody helped Gretchen carry her bags to Nedick's where she bought a donut and coffee. Gretchen and Homer stood side by side, but neither of them saw the other.

But each of them had already come up in the world. Homer had been the most colorless man in Missing Gap, Iowa.   He now was the most colorless man in New York City.   And as for Gretchen, well…you know the answer.

Nobody, seeing either of them, would have dreamed of the great success, the *éclat*, the social brilliance that would soon be theirs.

In New York, anybody can be popular.   You don't need to be rich.   You don't need to be talented.   You don't even need to be attractive.   Homer wasn't.   Gretchen wasn't. But you have to make the right contacts.   You have to *persevere*.

Homer began to persevere the very first day.   He got himself a room on East 33rd Street with a view of East 32nd Street and got a job running a passenger elevator at the O Lovable U Brassiere Company ("For The Woman Who's Hard To Fit") on West 29th Street. He figured it was a good way to meet people.

Unfortunately, nobody at O Lovable U paid any attention to Homer.   They crowded into his elevator and never saw he was there. The only conversation he ever had with a fellow worker was with lovely Clara Glotz, the bookkeeper.

Homer had read in *Reader's Digest* that the way to make friends was to be interested in other people's problems. Clara seemed to have problems. She was always staying late in the office alone with Mr. Mishkin, the president. One night she came down later than usual. Homer thought she looked tired.

"Been working hard?" he asked.

"Get lost!" she said.

The next day he was fired by Mr. Mishkin. He got a job running the elevator at Kleer-Sheer Hosiery Company. But nobody noticed him there, either.

Homer tried everything to become popular. He read all the magazine articles on the subject. Most of them were in women's magazines and had titles like "How To Drive Your Husband Wild In Bed." But he persisted. He found an article that said you should develop an interesting hobby. In the same magazine was an article on growing mushrooms. So he studied mushrooms.

But he never could figure out how to bring mushrooms into a conversation. He carried mushrooms in his pocket every day to work.

"Wanna see my mushrooms?" he asked Sadie Finch, the receptionist, one day, putting his hand in his pocket.

She gave him a strange look and got out at the next floor.

He answered an ad that said he'd be popular if he developed a torso like Charles Papadopolous ("No Longer A Ninety Pound Weakling!"). He bought a dumbbell, barbells, and a punching bag. But nobody noticed his burgeoning muscles. "Don't be a shrinking violet!" the ad said. One day he was riding on a crowded subway and a pretty girl was standing next to him. "Wanna feel my muscle?" he asked her. He clenched his arm and flexed his fingers.

She screamed. Somebody pulled the emergency cord. Homer was arrested as a sex offender and given a suspended sentence. To make matters worse, somebody had stolen his wallet.

According to an ad in the subway car, reading *The New York Times* would make him interesting. He read it avidly every day and night, including the obituaries.

"People are dying all the time," he observed to Mr. Missip, the treasurer, who was suffering from a heart condition.

"You should live so long," said Mr. Missip. End of conversation.

Still Homer persevered. He memorized verbatim entire stories from the *Times.*

One day he was standing on a street corner waiting for the light to change. He heard a man say something about Cuba. "That's ver-r-r-y interesting," Homer said. "Did you read Castro's latest speech?" And he quoted verbatim from it.

"Dirty Communist!" said the man. A woman swung an umbrella at him. Somebody screamed. Homer was arrested for disturbing the peace. He got off with a suspended sentence and a stern warning from the judge.

Still he persevered. He tried everything. He studied bridge, but nobody invited him to play. He went to museums. Even the attendants ignored him. He bought books on yoga, on Zen, and on hypnosis. He bought books on *Thirty-two Ways of Kissing* and *How to Be Absolutely Irresistible to Women.* But he was still lonely.

The only people he ever saw at his rooming house were the landlady, who always mistook him for a repairman; a roomer on the floor above, an old lady named Mrs. Hoggins, who thought he was the mailman; and a young lady named Margot La Marr who lived next to Mrs. Hoggins. Miss La Marr kept strange hours, so Homer didn't see much of her. She didn't seem to be lonely. She had visitors—always men—at all hours at night and sometimes by day. But when Homer passed her on the stairs she never noticed him. She looked right through him. She made him feel like a newel post.

Miss La Marr sometimes hung her laundry out to dry

on the fire escape. Homer had never seen black underwear before. He wished he dared to speak to her. He was sure she was an interesting person. He was sure they could be great friends. He could tell her all about mushrooms.

One day he saw an ad in *The Village Voice* announcing a "Get Acquainted Social For Lonely People. Find A Mate. Ten Dollars Admission. Ties and Jackets Required." It would be Saturday night at an address in the Village.

That night Homer read *The New York Times*, did a routine with the bar bells, dressed in his best clothes, and put some mushrooms in his pockets. Just as he was leaving to go to the party he noticed that a pair of Miss La Marr's black panties had fallen down and landed on the fire escape by his window. He picked them up and ran up the stairs. He paused before he knocked on her door. Strange sounds were coming from behind the door to her room. Surely she couldn't be crying? He knelt down and looked through her keyhole. He blushed. Miss La Marr had a visitor. Homer stood up with the panties in his hand. Just then Miss Hoggins passed on the stairs. "Men!" she exclaimed and slammed the door to her room.

Homer blushed and retreated to his own room. He wrote a note to Miss La Marr: "Dear Miss La Marr, I have your black panties, which you dropped. I'd be happy to return them at your convenience. Very truly, Homer T. Flack, your fellow roomer."

He ran downstairs and put it in her mailbox. Little did he know that this letter would turn out to be the turning point in his life. He was going to achieve fame and fortune beyond his wildest dreams.

Homer went to the party.

Gretchen Himmelheimer was also at the party. Like Homer and thousands of other bright, fresh young hopefuls who flock to the city, she'd found New York a lonely place.

She had a job as a filing clerk at the downtown office of the Amalgamated Insurance and Annuity Company. She shared an apartment with three young women who worked for the same company. They were typical New York roommates. One of them was a sweet young thing from Grand Chasm, Wyoming, who was in love with an absolute stinker who refused to help pay for her abortion; another was having an affair with a married man who loved his wife; and the third was a ballet student who searched through garbage pails in hopes of finding discarded jewelry.

Gretchen's office had only two employees. After her first month, her superior, who had held the same job for fourteen years, died of a heart attack, so Gretchen was alone. She was promoted from filing clerk to head filing clerk. After the second month, she was made office manager and Gretchen got a small raise, based on a misconception in the Personnel Office that she was someone else. Still, she told herself, she was on her way.

But Gretchen was lonely. She wanted romance. One of her roommates had committed suicide, one had gone mad, and the one who had gone through garbage pails had taken a job with the Department of Sanitation. That's the sort of thing that happens to roommates in New York.

Gretchen tried hard to be popular. She learned to play bridge. She learned to play tennis. She learned to shoot pool. Then she learned to shoot dice. She would have learned to shoot grouse if there'd been any grouse around. She took lessons at Arthur Murray. She got two cute poodles and walked them in Central Park. People knelt down to pet the poodles but didn't notice her. She wished she were a poodle.

She advertised in the dating columns in the papers. She got letters from teenagers who couldn't spell and older men who didn't want to waste their time on courtship. Gretchen was shocked by some of them. She wanted Romance. But she filed away some of the more outrageous letters for future consideration. "Just in case," she told herself.

Gretchen wore a Maidenform bra and tried to dream about it. She stocked up on the heavenly coffee. She washed her underwear twice a day and bought all the deodorants. She wore Kamasutra Perfume. She read about sex techniques in all the women's magazines. She learned to play the recorder. She joined a church group. Still nobody noticed her. She joined a writer's group but found she had nothing to write about. In desperation, she joined the Village Democratic Club. They decided she was a Republican because she wore a bra and heels. So she joined the Republican Club. They thought she was a Democrat because she looked like an intellectual. In desperation, she dyed her hair purple, but still nobody noticed her.

Finally, she saw an ad in *The Village Voice* that promised an evening of social fun for lonely people. It cost only ten dollars.

So she went to the party. It was in a crowded loft five flights up.

Homer T. Flack had arrived a few minutes earlier. He paid his ten dollars to a breathless hostess dressed in a peasant blouse, no bra, and a wide skirt. She had hair in her eyes.

"What do you do?" she asked.

"Fine, thanks. How do you do?" he answered.

"No, I mean what do you do. You know, like brain surgery, still life, sculpting, you know."

"I study mushrooms, read *The New York Times*, play bridge and practice yoga," he said. "Feel my muscle."

"How very interesting," she said. "Let me introduce you to some of these people. This is Tom billynancyloiselainepeterjohnbill'swithjoycenickharryand overthereisfrancis. This is Horace, folks. He eats mushrooms."

"Homer," he corrected.

"How very interesting." Everybody went back to talking and ignored him.

When Gretchen arrived, dressed in her best black dress, she was greeted by the same hostess.

"What do you do?"

"I play tennisbridgetherecorderandwritehaiku verse," Gretchen said.

"How very interesting. This is Tombillnancyloiselaine peterjohnbill'swithnancyandjoycenickharryandfrancis. Gretchen playsthehaikuisn'tthatinteresting?"

Everybody ignored her.

Gretchen saw Homer. Homer saw Gretchen.

Dear reader, no doubt you have surmised that these two would meet, and they would fall in love. Well, you're wrong. These two were so unappealing that they didn't even appeal to each other. They mutually turned their backs and didn't see each other again. At least, if they did they didn't notice it.

On his way home that night, Homer pondered suicide. It was one way to get people to notice him. But the police were waiting at his door. Miss La Marr had been the victim of a particularly horrible sex murder. They had Homer's note to her. Mrs. Hoggins had noticed him outside Miss La Marr's door. "He was pretending to be the mailman," she said. It was only circumstantial evidence, but Homer had a record.

Of course, Homer had an alibi. He'd been at the party at the time of the murder. The police checked. Nobody remembered him. The hostess had never heard of him.

Soon Homer's name was in all the papers, along with the lurid particulars of the crime. He was a celebrity. He got tons of fan mail. The first day he got eleven proposals of marriage, five of them from married women. Sandra McDowell, the noted columnist, interviewed him. "He has the look of the basic primeval," she wrote. "The type of man who is interested in ONLY ONE THING." The next day he received 351 love letters and 223 proposals of marriage. Twenty-two women volunteered to be his next victim.

After he was convicted, he got permission to marry one of the women who'd proposed by mail, an heiress named Sunny Smythe-Jones who had $853,000,000. TV news cameramen went to the wedding, held in Sing Sing Prison. Homer had *arrived.*

The day before Homer was to be executed, the real murderer confessed. Smythe-Jones sued for divorce. But Homer had become a hero. He was interviewed on television, and he hired a ghostwriter to write the story of his life. "The hardest job I ever had," the ghostwriter later confessed to a friend. "There's no *there* there."

The book became a selection of the Book of the Month Club and was on *The New York Times* Best Seller List. Hollywood filmed it. Homer ran for Congress on the Democratic ticket. "A policy wonk," the Republicans said. "He reads *The New York Times.*" This stigmatized him as an intellectual, but he was elected anyway.

And Gretchen? When she left the party in the Village, she stopped at a crowded Espresso bar for a latte. She sat opposite a pale, wan, scruffy young man with a beard, who offered her a smoke. She wondered how to start a conversation with him. "Do you play bridge?" she asked.

Just then the cops raided the place. There was an election coming up, and there'd been a scandal in the Department of Weights and Measures, so the mayor had ordered the police to crack down on street crime. The young man got away. He left a plastic bag on the table. The police noticed it, and hauled her in for selling marijuana. She was featured on the TV Evening News. "Zero tolerance for offenders," the mayor bragged. The public applauded. "Police Raid Reefer Den," the headlines screamed. They published her picture, dressed in black with a reefer in her hand.

Gretchen became a celebrity. The ACLU took up her case. Pot smokers staged a demonstration outside City Hall.

The police broke it up and dozens were arrested. "Zero tolerance for drugs," the mayor declared. He went up in the polls.

Newsweek published her picture, purple hair and all, and *Time* did a feature article on "How Safe Are Your Children?" Newspapers throughout the country ran cartoons showing her cringing before the towering figure of the mayor. It was an election year. Presidential, congressional, and senatorial candidates evaded questions about whether they'd ever smoked pot, but they all insisted that *The Laws of the Nation Had to be Obeyed.* Homer even quoted *The New York Times* to that effect.

The senior class of the high school in Flat Prairie, Kansas, invited Gretchen to speak at their graduation. The city council of Flat Prairie and twenty-seven other communities throughout the nation passed resolutions barring her forever from their precincts.

Gretchen spent six months in the county jail. Republicans denounced her short sentence. "Liberal coddling of criminals!" they claimed. "What Happened To the War On Drugs?"

The President and the Attorney General called for a life sentence without parole.

After Gretchen was released she was guest of honor at a large party sponsored by *The Village Voice,* whose readers had elected her Victim of Police Abuse of the Month. They presented her with innumerable prizes, including a book on Zen, three pairs of sandals, black tights, fifty-two sessions with an analyst, and a part in an Off-Broadway production.

She posed nude for *Playboy.* She rented herself out as a consultant to people uptown who wanted to give Hippie parties.

She charged a hundred dollars a party. Soon she was able to afford a new, roomy apartment. In gratitude, she invited the bearded young man who had given her the cigarette to become her new roommate. He takes dirty

177

pictures of her and sells them on the Internet. Gretchen is happy. She has many new friends.

If you ask Homer the secret of his popularity he'll hesitate, puff some smoke from his two-dollar cigar, and say "It's a matter of being in the right place at the right time."

Gretchen's answer is shorter.

"Just lucky, I guess."

THE PRICE
Martin Dodd

Small and frail, she can hardly hear.
Hair white and thin, her eyes are dimmed.
Her world, once wide, now is hemmed.
So old, so pale, so very dear.
Leaning close, I speak, "I came to see you."
A smile shapes her thin dry lips.
"That's nice," she says. Her head nods and dips.
Not sure of what to say or do,
I stroke her hand. Her brow knits in wonder.
She looks at me and her eyes show
A glint, ever so faint, I hope will grow.
Briefly, she looks like my memory of her.
"How are you?" I ask. She nods, says "Yes."
As if blowing on a spark, I caress her cheek.
But, the smile fades and her eyes become bleak.
I try again and again, but she says less and less.
She is unknowing sadness, a long life's price.
Her head droops. Age and loss have mostly won.
I want one moment, so I loudly state, "I'm your son."
With the slightest of smiles, she murmurs, "That's nice."

LEARNING TO SOAR
HELEN OLSON

A bird must flap its wings
Before it can soar
And when it soars
It does not waste energy
Flapping its wings.
Why do I always flap my wings
Even when I begin to soar?

~

CARING
HELEN OLSON

Invisible chains
Willingly carried
Thoughtfully added
Link by link
Year by year
Until death melts them
Into molten memories
To store and no longer carry.

SILENCE
ILLIA THOMPSON

Silence invites color
spreads white cloth
awaits yellow butterfly
to bestow a blush of gold.

Silence nods to
passing bluebird's song
watches notes of happiness
add pure light to canvas.

Silence holds its breath
as deer float from thicket
while essence soft as morning
ripples remembrance.

Silence reflects landscape
greens of young brush
heavy forest browns
silhouettes' darkness at play.

Silence knows the age of trees
without need to cut timber
to read concentric rings.

Silence knows where
mushrooms will appear
before spring rains.

Silence causes
    pauses of peace,
        so welcome
            at this moment

181

TRAFFIC

MARNIE SPERRY

"*And now, the news:* Traffic on freeways from Los Angeles to San Francisco remains at a standstill for the seventy-third day as commuters and other travelers remain trapped in their vehicles, due not only to the usual high volume of traffic now seen daily on this major thoroughfare, but also to various road-rage-induced incidents which, lately, are being enforced by freeway vigilantes.

"Sergeant Brooks of the California Highway Patrol, in a recent interview with this station's Tom Arrot, commented on the latest vigilante-type action: '*I really can't blame commuters for taking care of their own. CHP's hands are tied these days, there's just no way we can get to these crime scenes in time to stop them, let alone investigate them in any sort of timely manner. Back in the days of traffic-flow there's no way we'd put up with this, but I'm afraid this freeway situation is going to get worse before it gets better'.*"

Milton switched the radio off in disgust and turned on the small console television, where another newsperson was giving an update on the now-infamous 280 Tie-Up just south of San Jose. His daughter Susan was in that particular mess, had been for almost a week as she gamely made her way north to shop in San Francisco. A message left on the home machine said she was well and that she'd met the nicest man in the Mercedes next to her. Milton was proud of her tenacity, her willingness to go on with life in spite of the inconvenience of modern-day traffic, though he wondered briefly if Suze might follow the trend

182

—or tire tracks, as it were—of a growing number of young people called "lane lovers"—those who met, wooed and married their partners during one of these now common long delays on the roads. One of the churches had even started a "Motorway Ministry" bike brigade to perform such services. It was supposed to be "the" romantic thing to do these days, although he imagined the honeymoons left much to be desired. These days it was easy to get to know your lane neighbors pretty well, and he guessed he could see how young people, impatient to get on with life, might take their relationships to the next step.

His wife Celia had given up driving long ago after spending two days and nights on the San Diego Freeway next to a huge cemetery on Halloween night. Pranksters, celebrating All Hallows Eve, had played noisily among the gravesites and monuments, their lights casting eerie shadows across the well-manicured grounds. Thoroughly traumatized by the spooky echoes of ghostly laughter and lights emanating from the graveyard, she now refuses to even get into a car, and does all her shopping these days from catalogs, even placing grocery orders by telephone.

Milton's train of thought was interrupted by the ring-a-ding of an evening news bike making deliveries up and down his lane. He pulled a dollar from the dashboard money drawer and held it out the window. With a fluid exchange the deliveryman took his dollar and left a paper as he cycled past. He was glad to see it was Hal, back on his route after a run-in with a motorcycle gang several months ago. The motorcyclists couldn't really be blamed for the fight—they had each wanted a newspaper so Hal had to slow down from cycle to cycle to deliver each paper. The slow-down took quite a bit of time and it made him cross, and when he tried to pass half the gang without selling them their papers—well, they didn't like that much.

In the past four or five months Milton had seen or heard just about everything one could imagine happening on the roads—things that used to happen in the privacy of one's home, or in a hospital, or at least a motel room! Just a few weeks ago on his sales trip to San Francisco he'd attended the funeral of a man who happened to be a member of the parked-car poker party Milton had joined. The poor old guy had died in his car and no one even missed him till he didn't show up at the motor home two lanes over for the Tuesday night game. Bumper-to-bumper, the cars behind him had just pushed him along whenever the lanes moved forward a bit. The funeral service was held just a few cars ahead of Milton's own car, right at the old guy's station wagon so his lane-neighbors could attend. Modern Mortuary had taken care of all the arrangements, even provided flowers, and following the ceremony they gravely removed the body on a small three-wheeled trailer attached to one of their burial-bikes. Milton felt very touched as he noticed that cars up and down the freeway flashed their headlights once as a sign of respect and to say "farewell" as Modern Mortuary pedaled by with the old guy in tow. It was really a pretty decent send-off.

And last month Milton had helped during the delivery of twins in the back seat of a lovely old Ford Fairlane (he held the privacy curtain). There'd been a time he'd have felt thoroughly disgusted with a couple traveling with the wife so close to her due date, but these people had actually been on the road for over three weeks, trying to get back to their own home in Monterey after visiting her parents in Sausalito before their baby was born. Fortunately a MotorMedical trailer parked just past the Freeway Floral tent had both a doctor and a midwife on hand, and both attended the delivery to make sure all went well. That evening the happy couple paraded their new twin daughters up and down the lane, showing them off to the surrounding motorists and speculating on whether the two would be teething by the time they actually got home.

Milton saw a coffee seller's motorbike making its

way through lines of cars and rummaged through his glove box to find the green "vendor" flag which he hung from his car antenna, hoping the guy would have donuts this time. He'd long since finished his own thermoses of coffee, later joining long lines of other beverage consumers to take advantage of the convenient porta-potties that had become commonplace along California freeways. About a quarter mile ahead he saw the familiar Golden Arches flag indicating one of many MacDonald's trailers which, these days, maintained fully staffed kitchens that cooked around the clock for hungry commuters. He briefly felt the old resentment over commercial enterprises taking up one lane of the busy ten-lane highway, but the feeling just as quickly disappeared as his stomach rumbled for dinner.

The last ten years had seen such a surge in population growth that it was not uncommon for a person such as Milton to leave Monterey for work in San Jose early on a Monday morning and not even arrive at his office for a week or longer, so that such roadside conveniences had become necessities. Sure, he telecommuted when possible, but sometimes he simply had to get to the office. Alternate forms of transportation had suffered terribly as roads became mired in traffic, so there was no ingress or egress to airports, railroad stations, or even the once-speedy rail transit systems. A good many delivery services pay for all the hours their people spent on the road making calls to their customers. Quite a few companies now carried on business via telephone and computers from their employees' autos as they sat stalled for hours or even days from the office.

And it had only gotten worse as time went on. For this trip to San Jose Milton had left five, no — it was six days ago now, and it looked to be at least another two or three days before he even saw the outskirts of San Jose. These days throughout California as well as in most of the other heavily populated states, traffic progressed slowly forward on city streets and on freeways and highways.

"Road rage" had skyrocketed for a while, and woe to any unfortunate person who neglected auto maintenance or stupidly ran out of gas, as angry motorists surrounding the failed vehicle often converged on the hapless driver as an outlet for their traffic-induced frustration. Fortunately along with fast food restaurants lining the freeway came fast-gas refueling stations, although more than once Milton, having run out of gas himself, let his car get pushed slowly along in traffic by the motorists behind him, no one the wiser. Heck—they were all bumper-to-bumper anyway—for all he knew the cars in front and behind him were out of gas as well!

Lost in his reverie, Milton was startled when the car in front of him suddenly lurched forward—he couldn't believe that traffic was moving again so soon! It had only been a couple of hours since the last movement forward, a couple of car lengths then. All around him car doors were slamming and engines starting up, but before he could even reach for his ignition key a nasty green VW from the lane next to him popped into the space ahead, stopped, and two youngsters got out and began setting up a portable barbeque. Well, at least he had a different view for a while.

Oh good, here comes the library vendor...

SMOKEY'S GAME

PATRICIA MATUSZEWSKI

Smokey was a dusky pony with a flowing light mane and tail and melting chocolate eyes. Children had high expectations of him. After all, ponies are just the right size for kids, built low to the ground to ease the fall, patient, gentle, and sweet natured.

Smokey had expectations too. The kids who rode him should be small, light, and willing to tolerate unchallenging ambles, the direction and duration determined by him

One fall weekend far too many cousins came for a visit — and one cousin in particular, Butch. They all wanted to ride. This riding business was kind of a game played between unequal opponents. The kids just didn't know it. Visitors always took Smokey at face value, but the kids who grew up with him knew Smokey's apparent docility and patience hid great cunning. They called it "Smokey's Game."

He didn't resort to clumsy threats, such as baring his teeth or laying his ears back. His discouragements were far more humiliating.

For visitors, Smokey dusted off old tricks that the resident kids no longer tolerated. He would expand his gut when being saddled, then let out the extra air once the rider was mounted. The cinch slid, the saddle slipped, and the rider was left dangling sideways. Smokey was adept at the "cow kick," a kick out to the side, named for the experts at getting rid of those who tried to milk them. The only safe way to mount was standing sideways to his shoulder, facing his side and rear, an unnatural position, which, more often than not, landed inexperienced riders face first in the dirt.

Smokey had also been known to rear up and let the rider slip off, or to roll over to scratch his back—with the rider aboard.

On this particular visit, Smokey decided it was time for cousin Marilyn to graduate to a horse. He let her know this by walking up to an apple tree with a branch at just the right height to scrap her off his bare back. She got on again and he headed for the apple tree. So it went, until she decided she was far too old to be riding a stupid pony.

Valerie learned that open pit silage sticks like molasses and smells a lot worse than sewage. Butch danced around her laughing and holding his nose.

Roger was hijacked to the pigpen. When he whacked the pony's rump to get him to move away, Smokey was quick to obey, so quick that Roger sailed over the fence into the slop trough. Butch bent forward and moved towards Roger saying, "Oink-oink-oink."

Pete couldn't get Smokey to move at all. Butch yelled, "Kick him, kick him." Pete nudged him with his heels. Smokey put his head down, spread his legs, squatted a bit, peed slowly, and then stood immobile until Pete finally gave up and got off. Butch said, "You idiot. Kick him, I said, not tickle him. Watch me."

Butch was twelve and fat, much too big to be riding a pony, but Smokey was the soul of virtue as he mounted. Butch kicked him in the sides and yelled "Giddyap." Smokey moved forward. Butch yelled over his shoulder, "See? See? Ya just gotta let him know who's boss."

Butch reined left. Smokey walked straight ahead, speeding up. Butch reined right. Smokey walked straight ahead, even faster. Butch pulled back to stop him. Smokey trotted toward the farm pond. Butch sawed on the reins trying to make him turn left, turn right, stop, or slow down. Smokey ignored him.

The other cousins started laughing.

"Just like a boy," jeered Marilyn.

"Tickle him, tickle him," said Pete.

"Hee-haw, hee-haw," yelled Roger.

Smokey paused at the edge of the pond and then walked into the middle of it. Butch was up to his butt in cold, slimy water. Then Smokey stopped. Butch was scared now, and mad. He yelled. He kicked his heels into the pony's side. He cussed.

Smokey sat down, dumping Butch off backward.

"Shit!" Butch yelled, then sputtered and gagged, swallowing algae and muck.

Smokey ignored him, stood up, and ambled toward the bank. Butch tried to stand, but fell. He splashed around, falling again. Smokey climbed out, shook himself, and began to graze. The other kids were laughing and holding their sides. Roger was rolling on the ground.

Finally, Butch was able to stay on his feet, and began to slog toward the shore, dragging himself up on the bank red-faced and dripping water and weeds.

Valerie held her nose and said, "Oooo, peeww, 'pond scum'." The name stuck all through high school.

It was no coincidence that Smokey was put out to pasture soon thereafter. But, unlike so many of us, he retired at the top of his game.

~

CHARACTER

PATRICIA MATUSZEWSKI

Enough of adversity
to build character.
I have it or not.
Time to enjoy
the character I am.

"RUE" TURLOCK, PRIVATE EYE

MARTIN DODD

CHAPTER ONE: MEET TURLOCK

Rupert "Rue" Turlock is a *character*. I mean he is *supposed* to be a character. I dreamed him up as a fictional detective, but he acts like he dreamed me up. He sometimes "pops up" in my computer, or in my office, or other unlikely places. He questions my plots and actions, then "poof"—he's gone. He is alternately petulant, demanding, and intimidating. He even insinuates himself into my relationships. Friends ask, "How's Turlock?"

He's a "wannabe" Sam Spade *(The Maltese Falcon)* or Philip Marlowe *(The Big Sleep)*, both *a la* Humphrey Bogart (including a slight lisp, as in "shweetheart"). However, he is much underdressed and too lazy for either Spade or Marlowe; he leans more to Mike Hammer. He is studiously disheveled: suit coats that never match his pants; rumpled ties; and a stained, snap-brim fedora. He likes toothpicks, which he chews, wiggles, waggles, rolls across his lips, uses like a pointer, and regularly loses. He hasn't shaved in two days—never more, never less. I tried to honor all of this by naming him Philip Hammerspade, but he would not hear of it and named himself "Turlock." I asked him why and he said, "I like the town."

His relationships with women are chauvinistic and embarrassing. His vocabulary is wide—of the mark. He talks

190

as if he has to catch a bus and, when excited, he sometimes sprays spittle without apology (I think he believes it to be some form of spontaneous matter).

As for what it's like living with Turlock, let me share a recent encounter. I was at my computer checking my email, when I heard *POP!* I looked to my left and saw Turlock standing in the doorway. He hadn't changed a bit. He never does. A toothpick moved from side to side between his thin lips.

"Hi Turlock," I said with some trepidation.

"*Hi Turlock*," he mimicked in a sarcastic tone. He moved to my side, leaned over, and studied the screen. "Who is she? You ain't writing back and forth to a chick named 'Buzz' are you?"

"No, Buzz is my friend in Atlanta. What are you after, Turlock?"

He pulled up a chair and sat down facing me. "It's like this, 'Tappy-fingers' — "

"*Tappy-fingers?*"

"Yeah, you ain't like a real writer with a chewed pencil and a yellow pad. Hell, I'd accept a real typewriter. But a sissified computer keyboard? Tap-tap-tap-tap-tap — "

"Did you just pop in to insult me?"

"Naw, I'm here to protect myself. I wanna know where you're headed with your new 'pen pal' or 'word-processor pal' or whatever you call her."

"Oh — my new Buddy."

"Buddy? You call her '*Buddy*'? For Chrissake, I got myself an author that swaps notes with a chick he calls '*Buddy*'. Look at me, Wordman. Watch my lips. Try *my gal*."

"AOL calls 'em 'e-mail buddies', and she's not *my* — I wouldn't call her '*gal*' anyway. She's a new friend, and she's a very nice lady, and — uh, and — "

"And — and? She's got you stammering. And what?"

"Educated."

"*Ed-joo-cated?* Is that the best you can do? *Ed-joo-cated?* You're dancing like Howdy-Doody!" He fingered his toothpick as he nodded. "Yep, stammering and dancing. Yep, I can see where this is headed."

"Rue—"

"You only call me 'Rue' when you're trying to butter me up."

"OK, Turlock, but you don't know where any*thing* is headed or even if there is a *thing*. I don't know how you get it in your head—"

"From your head, shweetheart. I'm in the same head that you're using to write to your *ed-joo-cated buddy.*"

"Then, you should know everything that's going on, *Mister Snooping-in-my-head.*"

"That ain't easy. There's a lotta clutter up there, and you drank a year too long. There's too much space in your central tunnels, and there's some flak build-up—"

"It's plaque—and you're not making any friends. What's your point?"

"I don't get a clear picture of what's happening, just little hints, like a bad smell from an outhouse."

"*Like a bad smell...?* That's a *very* crude imitation of Marlowe."

He continued. "Who's Peggy McDill?"

"Peggy McDill! She was my girlfriend."

"How old?"

"Five or six."

His eyes bulged, and then narrowed. "You know it's bad enough being in the head of a hack writer, but you ain't some kind of *pervert*, too—are ya?"

"*Pervert?*"

"Well look at you. You gotta be seven days older than God, and you tell me you gotta girlfriend that's five years old."

"Turlock—you idiot. Peggy was my girlfriend *when I was five or six.* Now she's two months older than God, because—stop! You got me doing it."

192

"Don't blame me. I got neighbors up there among the clutter. Some of 'em don't even know how they got there — and some never sober up and others won't touch a drop."

"Pre- and post- AA," I offered.

He continued, "There's tricycles, Flexy-Racers, secret decoder rings, and Captain Marvel comic books. There's a panda bear with half his stuffing out — "

"That's it! Turlock, what do you want?"

"You don't have a fresh toothpick do you?"

I groaned, switched to the word-processor, and typed out "fresh toothpick."

Snap! One appeared in his hand. He smiled like Christmas morning. "Thanks."

"Don't mention it. Now — "

He leaned close. "What do I want?"

"Right."

"Remember when you were e-mailing that Japanese TV Chef?"

"Yes. What about it?"

"I got really tired of tempura, raw eel made me gag, and I got a kitchen full of Ginsu knives."

"What's that got to do with my new friend?"

"You're always picking up something from people that I end up having to deal with. Does this new *buddy* have a hobby, a favorite food, or some quirk that I'm gonna find in my life? I wanna be prepared. I got my standards, and limits — and issues."

"She writes poetry."

"Poetry! I can handle *that*. I met Shakespeare in there — " He tapped my forehead. " — and Poe, and Robert W. Service — *'The Northern lights have seen queer sights / But the queerest they ever did see / Was that night on the marge of Lake Lefarge / I cremated Sam McGee'.*"

"Very nice, but it's 'Labarge', Lake 'Labarge', not 'Lafarge'."

"Oh." He looked dejected.

"One of your issues?"

"Yeah. I'm kind of a perfectionist."

I looked at him. "It doesn't show. Anyway, poetry doesn't seem to fit you."

"Well, what else am I in for? Does she read mystery stories?"

"I doubt it, but if she does, she would probably like Agatha Christie."

He brightened. "I can do Christie. She's the best!"

"Oh, really? Better than Dashiell Hammett, Raymond Chandler, and Mickey Spillane?"

He stopped, stood, and stepped into the hall and looked in the full-length mirror. "Well, I do have a certain style." He moved back into the room. "But for Agatha Christie, I'll even modify my style. A chance to serve a real author —." He looked misty.

"OK. You got it. From now on, no sorta Sam Spade, no pretend Philip Marlowe, no hard-boiled Mike Hammer. From now on you are styled as — 'Miss Jane Marple'."

"M-M-Miss!" He spluttered and his toothpick landed on my shirt.

"Y-You gonna put me in a SKIRT?"

"You'll get used to it. She wears hats and ties. She's very tweedy."

Turlock was purple. "Marple is a, is a — FEMALE!"

"Most 'Misses' are."

"Not only that, she's really old — 'bout your age."

"Ouch — we're even." I removed the toothpick from my shirt and handed it to him. He jammed it in his mouth.

"No Marple?" He tested.

"No Marple."

"Poirot?"

"You'd really look silly with a moustache and monocle."

"Then gimme a better idea."

"As long as we're on English, how about a deerstalker, a Calabash Meerschaum pipe, a magnifying glass, a little cocaine, and your own amanuensis — "

194

"My 'man you insist – *what*'?"

"Forget it. I was thinking Sherlock Holmes. He's definitely English."

"Ummm, I dunno. I was never real sure about him and Watson." His face brightened. The toothpick came out, held in thumb and forefinger. "I've got an *idea*, a REAL English idea, all right – Ian Fleming, *double-oh-seven!*" He stood at attention and saluted, English style, palm out. "Bond – James Bond – 'On Her Majesty's Secret Service'."

I looked at his tie, the beard, and the clothes. "Oh, I don't think so. I really don't think so. Double-oh-seven is – *is not you.*"

"But, the gadgets, the villains, the *dames* – "

"No, Rupert."

"Why're you calling me Rupert?"

"To get your attention. I know – why don't we work some English comedy into your detective work? You could be John Cleese for a while instead of Bogart."

"Who's John Cleese?"

"You've got to know him from upstairs," I said, pointing at my head. "'Monty Python' and 'Fawlty Towers'-- a 'Fish Called Wanda' – funny movie. One guy stuffs french-fries in another guy's nose and eats his goldfish."

"*I ain't eating goldfish!*"

"Cleese doesn't eat the goldfish. Cleese is the guy who's caught nude in his client's house."

His eyes widened. "Oh yeah – yeah, I remember. He's trying to get it on with his girl. He turns her on by speaking Russian."

"That's right. You got it." I encouraged.

"I could do Cleese. The girl was real good looking."

"Jamie Lee Curtis."

He was smiling and waving his toothpick like a baton. "Yeah – nude, gettin' it on – I can do that. Hell, Boss, *gimme the right equipment and I'll be a standout!*"

I hit "reset" – *POOF!* He was gone.

CHAPTER TWO: THE BIG CREEP

Turlock was on a tear, demanding I write his story — "*or face the consequences.*"

"Like what?" I had asked.

His rejoinder was, "I know 'bout a very fragile hard-disk, belongin' to a hack writer — "

I got the hint. He told me some things he wants in the story. I took notes — let me see, oh — here: good description, a sexy female client, late 1940s, a dead body, and hints of his quick mind, all on the first page. Mmmmm.

Ready? Let's go.

(It begins.)

Rupert "Rue" Turlock, private eye, pulled the crumpled pack from his shirt pocket. He lit his last Camel and took an unfettered look at his battered, cluttered desk that was littered with an ever-present apple core, a glittering .357 magnum, a tattered find-a-word puzzle, six eraserless pencils, a 1946 calendar, a smattering of tootsie pop wrappers, and a very dead parakeet.

She was coming at four. He needed to be prepared. "Play it again, Sam," he said aloud. That wouldn't do, scratchy and too high. He was out of practice.

He removed his hat and put it on the desk, rose, and went to the bathroom. He peered into the mirror. The toothpick was perfect. A cheek-turning look showed him that the two-day stubble of beard was right for his job. He removed his tie and turned to the tie rack on the back of the door. He selected one, already tied, that had a gravy stain. He slipped it over his head, tucked it under his collar, and ran the knot up until it was two inches below the opened top button. A look in the mirror and a wink: "Well, Shweetheart — how 'bout it?" *Ah, good, bored, vague, but with authority — probing.* Satisfied, he returned to the desk.

He picked up his hat and placed it on the back of his head. He studied the rotting apple core that was next to his phone. He picked it up and tossed it into the waste can. He would have to replace it with a fresh one — in this business, image is everything.

He sat, facing the door, thinking about Automats. He hadn't been in one since he was a kid. *Put in a quarter, open the little door, and get your dessert — kinda like life.*

The office door slowly swung open. She stood framed in the oak doorway. He drank in her presence. Her yellow-blonde hair ended in pigtails around a heart-shaped face that was punctuated by a carmine-red, cupid's-bow mouth. Her proud breasts pushed insistently against her red off the shoulder, v-necked top that was sprinkled with strategically placed white polka dots.

He toyed with his toothpick and mused, *with that set of lungs she could stay under during commercials.*

The top was tightly tucked into black pinking-shear-ragged shorts that ended high-thigh, way above perfect knees. Her bare feet were finished by red toenail polish that matched her lipstick. Her rose-red lips pursed and formed a question. She spoke in a slow drawl that reminded one of catfish and fried okra. "Are you Turlock? *Rupert* Turlock?"

He winced. *There are some things you just can't forgive a mother for.* "Call me Rue," he growled.

She looked wide-eyed around the office. "Roo?" she asked. "Wheahevah is Kanga?"

He decided to skip Mother's next visiting day.

She moved to the chair across the desk from him. "Ah'm Daisy Yokum. You called me 'bout my husband's suicide. May I aye-isk, what is your interest?"

Turlock leaned back in his chair and put both feet atop his desk. "Sometimes, I get a feeling, Mrs. Yokum — a feeling like a melting Popsicle — I just gotta do somethin' about it. Your husband hired me to look into Kickapoo Joy Juice, Limited, a high-octane business deal gone sour. He didn't seem suicidal, just get-even angry. I schmoozed around and found a patch of dogs. Dogs that are barking 'fraud.' I had an appointment with him and showed up while the police and coroner were there."

He was watching her breasts for an increase in breathing. He didn't get a rise from her — that is, she showed no concern.

Daisy sat motionless for a minute then spoke, "Li'l Abner was jes' a big creep. What do ya want from me?"

TO BE CONTINUED...

I exited the word-processor.

POP! Turlock stood beside me.

"That's *it,* Wordman? *To be continued...?*

"That's the way it's done, Turlock. You leave the reader hanging. It's called a page-turner."

"What happens next? She's a looker."

"I don't know yet." I rose from my chair and moved around him. "I got a date."

"A date! Then, I'll finish it myself." He sat down in front of the computer.

"Goodnight, Turlock." I reached past him and turned off the power strip.

"Leave now and loooose meeee." His words died away like a passing train, as he faded from view — leaving only a toothpick behind.

CHAPTER THREE: TURLOCK RETURNS

It had been several months since Turlock responded to any of my opening lines. *The Big Creep* was unfinished. The problem (well, *his* problem) was that I had taken up with a certain lady. You could say she and I were an *item*. Turlock? Frankly — he was jealous.

I was walking to my English literature class at Monterey Peninsula College when I spied him. He was leaning against the building near a classroom doorway. His back was to me. I knew him at once. His hat was pushed back on his head. His coat and pants didn't match.

I walked faster, and when I was about twenty feet away, I spoke, "Turlock — is that you?"

He flinched, hunching his shoulders, but he didn't turn or reply.

"Turlock, I know it's you." I walked around to face him. I stopped and stared.

He was wearing one of those ridiculous gag masks. Not really a mask, but you know — the glasses with big nose, furry eyebrows and moustache. However, a dead give-away was the toothpick sticking out of the corner of his mouth.

"Turlock —," I spluttered somewhere between a choke and a giggle, " — what's with the get-up?"

"Geddup? Geddup? Votta you mean, geddup? Have vee met? The name is Putzmann — Murray Putzmann."

I just stared for a moment then shook my head. "The name is Murray Turlock. Your accent's sillier than your *geddup*. What are you doing?"

"Sveetheart — though vee don't know vun anudder — I'm takink creative vritink."

"What are you vritink? — I mean *writing*?"

"I'm lookink for a new vriter."

"I'm your vriter."

"Wuz, Sveetheart, er, vuz — though vee don't know vun anudder."

199

I grimaced. "Stop it, Turlock. You're being *very* politically incorrect."

He spoke in a hoarse whisper, "You're goink to blow my coverrr. Come vid me." He turned from the door and walked toward a sitting area under a large oak tree. He sat on a bench and faced me. "Whaddaya want? Make it snappy. I'll be late for class."

"Can you take off the nose? I can't talk to you when you look like a bad ethnic joke."

He removed the glasses and nose and slipped them in his pocket. He grasped his toothpick with his thumb and forefinger. He twirled it in his lips for a moment, then removed it and pointed it at me, sorta jerky, stabbing back and forth. "Ya know, you got a lotta nerve. You ditch me for a skirt. I'm left in literary limbo. I'm—"

"*Skirt?*" I interrupted.

He popped the toothpick back in his mouth and continued, "I'm without a voice, without action, without being, just without—gone, forgotten, and you? You're playing Romeo—"

"*Skirt?*"

He didn't pause, "—and writing? What are *you* writing? Poetry—*poetry* for Chrissakes!" Spittle flew like exclamation points. "I give you a shot at an Edgar—and whaddaya do? You take up with a bunch of poets!"

"I thought you liked poetry."

"Ya got somethin' on ya." He wiped his exclamations from my jacket. "*Pebbles Writers Group*, ain't it? Poets. I'm gonna buy you a beret."

"They're not all poets. Pat writes mysteries, and Harold writes kind of Huck Finn stories, and Ken writes some hard-boiled stuff—"

"And Georgia writes Jewish-mother, chicken-soup stuff."

"That's not very respectful, Turlock."

"Respect! You gonna talk to me about respect? I'm a character who's been *dissed* by his author. I'm Moses drowning in the Red Sea. I'm Elijah without a match. I'm Phantom without an Opera, while you're spooning, mooning, and *rooning* my life. You're two-timing, and got me rhyming. It's — it's *character abuse!*" The last he shouted and in the process spit his toothpick into the grass.

"Turlock?"

He snarled at me.

"Rue —"

"What?'

"I'm sorry."

"You sure are."

"I'm apologizing."

"For what? Desertin' your best friend or being a lousy author?"

"Both."

"Do you mean it?"

"Yes."

"Then help me find my toothpick." With that he was on his hands and knees searching in the grass.

"Here, try one of these," I said. I reached in my pocket and pulled out a small vial of plastic toothpicks. "My skir — I mean my lady gave them to me. They're molded with thin, flat points on one end and a sort of tiny brush on the other — a perfect toothpick."

Turlock straightened up, still on his knees. He took the vial and pulled out one of the picks. He held it up, squinting at it. He looked at me. "What do you want me to do with this?"

"It's a toothpick."

He placed the pick back in the vial and handed it to me. He stood and placed his hand on my shoulder. "That ain't a *toothpick*, friend — *it's a machine*. I'm not looking for a pocket-dentist. I'm trying to keep a professional image. An image you seem to have forgotten. An image that you claim to have created — not that you could maintain it without my help — a style, a flair, a mystique, a certain *panacea*."

"Panache."

He ignored me. "The toothpick is my signature. My kind of toothpicks are at every greasy diner. They hold the pickle to the hamburger. You can dig wax out of your ear with them. They get soft and splintery when you chew them. I'll take them flat or round. I'm not too picky. Now, if you really want to help, you'll help me find my real friend — my *only* friend — *my toothpick.*"

"Turlock — ?"

"Yeah?"

"I think you're standing on it."

MY VICIOUS LOVER
HELEN OLSON

Let me go my vicious lover!
Let me break from your insatiable hunger,
Your binding caress
How did I come to adore your deadly charms,
Your distractions with no end
The satisfaction of attention, entertainment, and praise
Dissolves always too quickly
It cannot give the eternal rapture
Of a tiny luminous dewdrop,
Or a contented cat asleep in my arms
I want to go, my vicious lover!
I want to flee yet I know not where or how
You have always been there to provide
Like the master for the slave,
The "gentleman" for the mistress
I feel the pull of my need to care, provide, respond
Like the earth does to gravity
Yet the discomfort is strong as well
When your incessant charms are slighter
I feel the refreshing breeze of my own spirit stirring,
Flowing between myself and the world of my conscious
imagination,
Gently pulling us together in joyful repose
Let me go, my vicious lover
Your charms have tired my body, mind, soul
Loosen your grasp on my subservient being just enough
So I can reach the glorious essence
The true tonic for my soul's real life

CONJECTURE
ILLIA THOMPSON

Sweeping dirt off earth
must have been pioneer women's work
in wooden cabins
where wind played notes
through spaces between boards.

With brooms of brush
gathered from sparse growth
in wide wilderness
the women knew sweeping
would never be finished.

Maybe that helped
to keep them alive
through storms and drought,
the knowing that they would
always be needed.

Each pile gathered
taken outside to float as dust
to land as loam on barren fields
perhaps to become fertile soil
promised renewal.

Each set of hands
in perpetual readiness
hungered to serve
grace before meals.

YOU'LL BE SORRY

PATRICIA MATUSZEWSKI

Kara pushes through the swinging door to the kitchen, slams her book bag down, and knocks over her orange juice, angry, intent. "I'm sixteen now Mom, sixteen, and you treat me like I'm six. I never get to do anything fun. I might as well be dead. You'd be sorry then."

Suddenly I'm seven years old, thinking, *She can't be dead. Just last Saturday was her sweet sixteen party,* as I stare at the sunshine hair that frames a perfect oval face against the white satin lining of her coffin. Her dress, worn with a pearl necklace and earrings, is the color of spring sky. Her blue-violet eyes, so clear and fine, are closed.

Mom puts a hand on my shoulder, pushes gently, and whispers, "Annie, love, move along. You're holding everyone up."

I move forward blindly, take my seat, and hear not a word of the service. My head fills with the sound of my heartbeats. My right eyelid begins to twitch like there's a worm wriggling around in it. The scent of lilies is suffocating.

Sounds of people trying to be quiet fill the church – little rustles of settling, fabric slithering across wooden pews, whispers, sniffles, coughs, sighs. Organ music settles over our heads, pushing down. A fugitive ray of sun cuts the chill overcast, streams through the stained glass rose window, and drapes the casket in light jewels.

This is my first funeral. No one tells me how she died. They are protecting me, but I heard the whispers.

After the funeral, Mom says to Aunt Fran, "It's so sad. She was so young. But what was she to do?"

"It's still a sin."

"But whose sin?" Mom says, then, nodding toward me, "Shh, later — little pitchers have big ears."

Pitchers with ears?

Mom starts to move pots and pans around, pretending she's going to cook, and says, "Annie, you can go over to Melanie's until dinner."

I run out, purposely letting the screen door slam.

Melanie, my best friend, says, "My Dad told my Mom he heard that dead girl killed herself. Mom says the girl's dad or her boyfriend killed her. Then they saw me hanging around and stopped talking about her and asked me about school."

"Maybe she was in an accident."

"Maybe she just died," Melanie says shrugging, losing interest.

If she can die so young, anyone can, I think. That thought stays with me for a long time.

When I was sixteen, her age, I often thought of how she looked in her coffin, so beautiful, so serene. I remembered that everyone was sad and sorry, so very sorry. I wondered, did she say it? You know, "You'll be sorry when I'm dead." I wondered because I thought it often. Sixteen fears and favors death.

* * *

I ignore the orange juice, now dripping onto Molly, our ever-hopeful under-table mutt. I catch Kara in a sudden fierce hug. She drops her head, flustered and embarrassed. These days, angry words hold us at arm's length. "Oh yes sweetheart, I would be sorry. More than you know. But you still can't go this time. We'll talk about how to make it work next time." She knows she can't go, but feels better for the venting.

She escapes in a relieved rush as we see the bright flash of the school bus turning the corner a block away.

When she opens the door the sun rushes in, catching her in shimmering outline. I whisper to that other girl, *"You can leave now, we'll be okay."*

NIGHT REFUSES TO SLEEP
ILLIA THOMPSON

My sister and I sort
Mother's belongings
at the walnut dining table,
piled high with photograph albums.
Divide our heritage, poignant glimpses.

We weigh each picture carefully,
ask where it wants to travel next.
Residue blackens our hands
as dark pages crumble, tear,
or even resist our deliberate touch.

My first wedding day shows no clue
of future's sharp tear of divorce.
Further on, our boy and our girl
tumble for a playful decade
between heavy embossed covers.

This slice of love no longer here,
still cuts deeply into my flesh
fresh burning under silken scar
thought forever healed with another marriage
and the sheer gladness of living.

BY COINCIDENCE

MARTIN DODD

The last time I had sat on that bench was with Eve, two years previous — our last Valentine's Day together. She died seven months later. I guess I'd gone to Lovers Point, two years later, on another lovers' day, to somehow connect. I hadn't really planned it.

I sat looking across Monterey Bay. It was twilight, but people were still climbing on the huge rocks immediately to my left that formed the end of the Point. About a hundred yards to my right, next to several large cypress trees, the Old Bath House Restaurant sat on a bank thirty feet above a small beach. Beyond the restaurant, and to the left, were the Victorian bed and breakfast inns that lined Ocean View Boulevard.

I'd been there a couple of hours reminiscing about the many times Eve and I visited the Point and nearby restaurants since we moved to the area over thirty-five years ago. In the early years those had been family outings. Later, after the kids grew up, it was just the two of us.

There was a chill in the air, and I started to leave. A lump swelled in my throat. I pulled the small notepad from my jacket pocket. I would re-read the poem I had written that morning and then go.

LONELY VALENTINE

To be, on this day,
And not to love,
Is but death while I live.

208

My breath is shallow,
And stillness rings in my ears.
My soul is wingless,
And existence is only a duty.

"Whatcha doing mister?"

I looked up. A boy of ten or so was standing before me. He had red hair and was dressed in a cap, sweater, and jeans — all green.

"I'm just thinking, young man."

"I'm a boy," he said. "Can I think with you?"

Before I could say, *"Please do,"* he plopped onto the bench beside me.

"Where'd you get your red hair?" I asked.

"It's always been this way. How come yours is white?"

"Because I'm old," I replied.

"Why'd you get old?"

"Well, it just happened, while I was waiting for something else."

"I'll never grow up," he said.

Just wait, I thought, then asked, "Are you visiting here?"

"Yes."

"Where do you live?"

"Second to the right and then straight on till morning."

Kid talk, I thought then asked, "What's your name?"

"Peter. What's yours?"

"That's a coincidence. My name is Peter."

"What's a coincidence?"

"Well, some people say coincidences are God's way of staying anonymous."

"Huh?"

"Well, it's when things happen at the same time that can't be explained easily. Like, we just met. There's only the two of us and we're both named 'Peter'. It's just kind of strange."

209

"Strange is nice," he said, "but it'd be nicer if we were both boys."

"That'd be a miracle. It'd be easier to fly."

"I can teach you to fly."

"You can't teach an old dog new tricks."

"Huh?"

"It means I'm too old to learn anything."

"It's easy," he said.

"Flying?"

"Yes. You just think lovely thoughts," Peter explained, "and they lift you up in the air. Try it."

I leaned back, closed my eyes, and said, "'Freedom's just another word for nothing left to lose'."

"That doesn't sound very lovely."

"OK. How about, 'To love another person is to see the face of God'?"

I heard a woman's voice. "Pardon me?"

I opened my eyes. The woman standing before me had a pleasant, and somewhat puzzled, expression. She also looked familiar.

I smiled. "I was learning to fly." She looked even more puzzled. I started to say, "*This boy was...*" Then I realized Peter was gone.

She stared at me for a moment then said, "I know you. You're Peter Newman, aren't you?"

"Yes, and you are — ?"

"Wendy Stiller. We were members at St. James together, what — um, twelve years ago."

I stood. "Of course. You and uh — your husband moved east didn't you?"

"Barry. Yes, New London, Connecticut."

"How is Barry?"

"He passed away last year."

"Oh, I'm sorry." I paused. "I lost my wife recently, too."

"How sad — my condolences."

"Thank you. What brings you back here?"

"Barry and I were married here at Lovers' Point on

210

Valentine's Day forty years ago. I've been dreading the thought of this anniversary and being alone. So, on impulse, a couple of days ago I made travel arrangements and here I am. I guess I'm trying to make some connection."

"That's a coincidence. I'm here for sort of the same reason. Are you staying nearby?"

"I'm at Grand View Inn—over there." She nodded toward the boulevard. "Funny thing, I've just returned from Carmel in time for dinner, and I saw a firefly out by the street."

"*A firefly?* In Pacific Grove? It's too cold."

"Sounds strange, doesn't it? Brightest firefly I ever saw. I tried to get close to it, but it kept flitting away. I followed it, and here I am, three blocks from the Inn. I was following it when I thought you spoke to me. Didn't you see it?"

"No. I was talking to a boy. And he seems to have disappeared."

"Is that him?" Wendy pointed towards the rocks.

It was getting dark, but I could see young Peter standing on one of the rocks, looking out to sea. There was a light flitting around his head.

"There's the firefly, too!" Wendy exclaimed. "Do you see it?"

"Yes." Then, I faintly heard a tinkling bell. "Do you hear a bell?"

"Yes, I think I do," she responded. "Perhaps it's wind chimes at the restaurant."

"It sounds more like the dinner bell my mother had when I was a boy."

"Mmm, it *does* sound like a dinner bell."

"Well, speaking of that, would you—would you like to join me for dinner?"

"Why—yes. Yes, I would. That's a lovely thought."

~ *The Beginning* ~

WELCOME TO THE REAL WORLD

PETER HOSS

Gary received his first invitation to the Drink and Dine with the Good Old Boys Club at their monthly meeting. His boss, the bank manager, congratulated him and told him this was the first sign of upward mobility in the business community. It was particularly impressive for a young man only twenty-eight years old and six years out of college.

The bank manager explained that Fred would be the host, and that Fred was the dominating force in the Good Old Boys Club. Fred was the owner of the largest locally owned business in town, and the wealthiest man in town, a self-made man, a good man to meet..

After the Good Old Boys assembled, Fred told a joke. It was about an Iraqi division that sent a scout over a hill. The scout reported seeing one U.S. Marine. The division commander decided to investigate, and after doing so came back quaking with fear and announced to his troops that they would have to surrender, because he reported that there were two Marines.

The Good Old Boys laughed uproariously. Gary did not laugh. Fred noticed and looked at Gary.

"Didn't you get it?"

"I get it but I do not think it is funny. The war is unnecessary and unjustified. Our nation was wrong in instigating it."

Gary was an outspoken and zealous opponent of the war in Iraq. He had been waiting for an opportunity to try to

212

convince influential people that the war was wrong and ill-advised.

He considered himself well informed on the issues, and had read extensively about the war. He thought, somewhat impulsively, that this might be an opportunity.

But Fred cut him off before he could get started.

"Don't you support our troops?"

"Of course I do. I support the troops, but I do not support the war."

"You cannot support the troops and not support the war."

"I believe you can."

"Patriotic Americans support the war. America, love it or leave it."

Fred was getting red in the face, talking loudly. Gary was getting upset.

The assembled Good Old Boys watched in stunned silence.

Gary responded, "I am in a place where no one wants to hear what I have to say. I am not leaving America, but I will leave here."

When Gary arrived at work the next morning, there was an urgent message to see his boss, the bank manager, who started talking without even saying good morning.

"You really pressed Fred's button last night."

"You heard about it."

"From about ten people, up until midnight."

"I was just expressing my right of free speech. Can't I still do that in this free country? Who is this man to say I can't do it? He is a real bully. I guess he thinks he can act that way because he owns half the town."

The bank manager continued.

"I need to tell you a little about Fred, which I thought everyone knew. He is a highly decorated Vietnam veteran, a Marine platoon leader. He is very tough and very brave. His troops admired him and were in awe of him. I have talked to several of them. After Fred came home from Vietnam, he was marching in a parade in his Marine uniform with all his medals. An unwashed hippie came up to him and spit on the medals. It took five of Fred's buddies to pull him off the hippie and stop him from dismembering him on the spot. Fred was very grateful to his buddies, because he certainly would have killed the guy. Fred realized he had a problem with anger, which he needed to control. He took anger management courses and became more peaceful. However, he is still adamant about the subject of war. I should have warned you. There is more you should know. Fred is a very tough businessman, but there is another side to Fred that is not so well known. He lives very modestly. He is not married and has no family. He has given away hundreds of thousands of dollars, usually anonymously. He does not want anyone to know about his philanthropy because he does not want anyone to think he is a softie. He likes to project a tough exterior. I know this because I am his banker. There might be a chance to salvage this if you go and apologize to Fred. He has a soft side."

"Apologize? For what? All I did was express an opinion about something I strongly believe in. Don't I have the right of free speech in a free country? How can we ever stop wars unless people speak out?"

"Of course you have the right of free speech. No one is going to put you in jail or kill you for what you said. But, the exercise of free speech has consequences you have to accept. Fred is not required to accept your opinion. You embarrassed him at his party, to which you were an invited guest. You made him look foolish. Everyone I talked to thought you were rude and arrogant."

The tone of the manager hardened noticeably. "There is another aspect of this you need to consider in the real world. Just as you have the right to say to Fred whatever you wish to say, Fred has the right to choose what bank he wishes to patronize. You need to get off your high horse, swallow your pride, and do what you have to do to prevent this bank from losing its biggest customer."

"You mean Fred would change banks over this?"

"I cannot be sure. I cannot take a chance. I am just a branch manager. My superiors would be very unhappy if we lost Fred's account."

"You would fire me because I spoke my convictions?"

"I don't think I would have much choice. It would be my job or yours, most likely both our jobs. You would not last if Fred pulled his accounts and I was fired because I would not fire you. Besides, I have a family, kids in college, and 53-year-old bank managers are lining up right and left looking for work in this economy. Have I made myself clear?"

"Indeed you have. You don't have to fire me. I quit."

The manager responded. "You need to calm down, think it over. You have a promising future here if you can make peace with Fred. Talk to your wife. Your resignation will not be effective till noon tomorrow. It is not too late to change your mind, which I urge you to do."

Gary went home and told his wife what happened. She was upset.

"Gary, this is awful. I love our new home so much I wake up singing. The kids love the neighborhood and have made wonderful friends. The schools are good. Isn't there any way we can stay?"

"How can I compromise my beliefs? We may have to go somewhere else where my beliefs will be accepted."

"Where will that be? What makes you think it will be different anywhere else? You cannot run away from the real world."

She started crying and went into the bedroom. Gary walked into the back yard. The kids were playing on their new swing set. They told him how much they loved their new house, their new friends and the new neighborhood, and how much they loved him.

215

Gary went into the bedroom and tried to console his wife. She pleaded through her tears, "Why couldn't we contribute financially to anti-war causes? Why do you have to be on the front lines? Why do you have to ruin a career? I'll stand by you, but must you do this? Isn't there another way?" He could not console her. She would not stop crying.

Gary called the bank, asked the manager for Fred's number and told him he needed more time to think.

He picked up the phone and cradled the receiver in his hands. He could see the kids playing in the yard out the window and hear his wife crying. His heart was beating, his mind racing. He thought to himself, *this had to happen sooner or later. Welcome to the real world. The real world is not black and white, it is a kaleidoscope.*

DO YOU LOVE ME?

WALTER E. GOURLAY

"But what if they don't like me?" she asked.

"Don't worry. To know you is to love you," he answered, giving her a hug and patting her rump.

"This is a stupid idea. Coming here."

"Just be yourself, sweetheart."

"I am myself. That's the trouble. Myself is nobody. Nobody ever listens to me. Nobody likes me. I'm just nobody."

"You're somebody to me."

"That's because you don't know me."

"For God's sake, Gloria, stop feeling so sorry for yourself."

"See? You don't like me."

"I love you for God's sake. But sometimes you're a bit too much. You—" He fell silent.

"I what?" She stood still. "I what? Say it."

"You drive me crazy."

"So you don't like me. So let's forget about the whole thing." She turned away.

He grabbed her arm and pushed her toward the door. "God damn it, pull yourself together!"

"Alan, stop! I'm going home."

"Okay, okay. Go home, damn it."

"Will you call me?"

"Yes, I'll call you."

"Tonight?"

"Yes."

"As soon as you get home?"

"Yes. I will."

"Promise?"

217

"I promise."

The door opened. Alan's mother, Wilma, looked out. "Alan! And this must be your bride-to-be! Oh, Gloria, we're so happy to meet you! Alan's told us so much about you! Alan, she's beautiful! Do come in!" The young couple walked in to the party.

"People, I want you to meet Gloria, Alan's intended. Isn't she lovely?"

There followed a round of introductions and congratulations, Gloria close to Alan's side.

"Are you sure they liked me?" Gloria asked as they walked to their car.

"They absolutely loved you, Gloria."

"They were just pretending." She looked at him beseechingly. "Alan, do you really love me?"

"Of course I do."

"Besides the stuff in bed?"

"Of course."

He hugged her and gave her a kiss.

"You really, truly love me?"

"I really truly love you."

"Not just in bed?"

"Not just in bed."

"Really?"

"Really."

"You're telling me the truth?"

"I'm telling you the truth."

She gripped his arm and they walked to his car in silence.

"I'll take you home," he said.

"You don't want me to stay with you?"

"I'm pretty tired tonight," Alan said.

"You don't love me."

"Of course, I do."

"You're tired of me."

"Of course not," he said, realizing that for the first time he'd just lied to her.

SATURDAY MORNING

KEN JONES

Sarah stretches, yawns and opens her eyes slowly to the brightness of the morning. She's alone in the bed. She listens to the muted sounds of the shower from behind the closed bathroom door. Forcing herself to move, she tosses back the covers and walks stiffly to the downstairs bath. The cold water feels sharp on her face. She combs her hair with wet fingers and tightens her robe sash.

In the empty kitchen, she pours a cup of coffee and sorts through the sections of the morning paper that are spilled across the kitchen table. She wills herself not to think about yesterday's design review, or her staff meeting looming on Monday. The coffee and the sun through the window over the sink warm her as she absently gazes at the headlines. Down the block a dog barks and children laugh. The coffeepot clicks on, then off again. The refrigerator's icemaker fills itself. Just another Saturday morning, she thinks, no different from any other in the string stretching back over the last twenty years.

The screen door bangs as Josh, her youngest, comes in from the back yard. "Found one of your earrings, Mom," he says, and drops a small trinket onto the table.

"Thank you, dear." She picks up the earring and rubs it lightly between her fingers.

"Found it under the seat while I was looking for my mitt in the car."

"Sit down, I'll make you some breakfast."

"Naw, I got practice this morning."

"You *have* practice this morning."

219

"That's what I said," said Josh, smiling—an old joke. "Okay, I *have* practice. Anyway, I'm late and I gotta go." He lifts his arms to shield himself from her mock glower.

"Terry's coming over after practice. We're gonna play Space Commander."

"You *are going* to play Space Commander."

"Is there an echo in here?" He ducks again. They both laugh.

"Okay, smarty-pants. I'll fix lunch for the two of you. How about tomato soup and grilled cheese sandwiches?"

"All *right!*" He brushes a quick peck against her cheek and starts for the door.

"Here, eat something now." She throws a banana to him. He catches it big-league style and runs out, letting the screen door smack shut behind him.

Sarah sips her coffee and considers the earring.

She used to be able to see the future. Though not in the crystal ball mystical sense, she had always had a vision of where her life was going. Her vision helped keep her up on the down days, and gave her a sense of working toward something. She gazes into that future now but can't see a thing.

The sound of footsteps pulls her thoughts back to the present. Lynn, middle child, fashion queen, comes into the kitchen, apparently from a wind-tunnel test. She pulls a carton of orange juice from the refrigerator, pours a glass, and sits at the table sipping the juice.

"What happened to your hair?" Sarah asks casually.

"I finally got it right," Lynn answers without eye contact, as usual.

"Interesting. I thought perhaps we all could go to a movie this afternoon."

"Can't. Told Jeanie I'd meet her at the mall. That new music store's opening today and some guys from *Body Parts* are supposed to be there."

220

"Body Parts?"

"The band, Mom," Lynn says slowly, with a heavy sigh.

"Oh, right. The band. Well, you can't miss *that*," Sarah says, immediately sorry for the sarcasm in her voice. Her daughter doesn't seem to notice.

Lynn finishes her juice, gives her mother a quick kiss and a rare smile and hurries out of the kitchen.

Alone again, Sarah tries once more to look into the future. It used to come to her so easily. Over the years, though, the images had gradually faded into a shapeless blur. So gradually, in fact, she hardly noticed the change. She sees nothing recognizable there now. Nothing good, nothing bad. Only nothing. How can I get it back? she ponders. The question echoes in her mind, returning only slightly altered. Do I *want* to get it back?

"Mom, have you seen my acceptance letter?" David, her oldest, calls from the hallway. "I've looked everywhere!"

"It's in your blind spot," she says as he joins her in the kitchen.

"My blind spot?"

"Directly in front of you at eye level. Do those people at Stanford know they've accepted a blind student?"

"Mom..."

"Look on the fridge."

The letter is held to the door with a magnet. David gives his mother a stage glare, removes the letter, reads it and smiles.

"Monday's going to be a big day, David. Are you ready?"

"Are you, Mom?" A small silence passes quickly through the kitchen like a breeze.

"Would you like to go to a movie this afternoon?"

"I'd like to, Mom, but I'm going up to Santa Cruz today. Brad just moved into the dorm and he wants me to check it out."

Sarah nods and takes a sip of her coffee. "Are you sorry you're not going to Santa Cruz with Brad?"

"Maybe a little. But Stanford is just so cool. Brad wishes he were coming with *me*. He's smart enough. They just can't swing it, you know?"

She nods again. "Well, drive carefully. See you for dinner?"

"Sure." He kisses her on the forehead and leaves.

Three great kids, she thinks. How lucky I am.

In the future she used to see so clearly, the kids all graduate from college, find fulfilling jobs and start families of their own. She and Isaac grow old together and enjoy the success of their children and their memories of a life built and spent together. She can still see the kids clearly. But when she looks for herself and Isaac now, the images fade.

She picks up the earring: a beautiful teardrop ruby with intricate gold lacing. She's seen it before, of course, but not in *her* jewelry case. The last time she saw it, it hung from a pale shell-like lobe some twenty years younger than her own. It flashed at her from behind silky blond locks at the company's New Years Eve party last year. The ear it had hung from belonged to one of Isaac's research assistants. Vicky, or Trixie, or something.

Sarah's not surprised as she gazes at the bauble resting in her palm. It's merely the most recent other-womanly thing to turn up in a pocket, the glove compartment, or car seat. She wonders if these women didn't leave them behind on purpose, the way the troops used to write messages and sign their names on the bombs to be dropped on the enemy. These small sparkly or sometimes silky bombs had caused serious damage in her life once. This latest, however, has very little effect. She wonders if the explosives are getting weaker, or if there is simply nothing left to destroy.

She hears Isaac in the hall and cups her hand around the earring. He strides into the kitchen smelling of soap and aftershave. He pours himself a cup of coffee and sits at the table, picking up the paper. She watches him scan the page. He could be the only person in the room.

Sara sips her coffee, waits for a look, a nod. Finally she says, "Where are you going all dressed up?"

"Have to meet some people."

"You didn't mention you had a meeting today. It's Saturday. I thought we could go to a movie."

"Just came up."

Sara feels the familiar tension begin to build inside her. She braces for the usual blend of sadness, anger, hopelessness, and frustration that she knows will overtake her if she lets it. Her stomach feels hollow at the thought of starting the day with a fight. She waits for the rush of feelings, but it doesn't come. She wonders if she's just too tired to push anymore. No. She actually feels strangely refreshed. As she regards Isaac she can feel the tension leave her. She sips her coffee and glimpses the future again. An image is beginning to form in her mind. The anxiety that used to accompany her attempts to make out what her life means is absent on this Saturday morning. She can't see much detail, but she sees the path clearly. She feels light, unhurried, secure.

"You'd better pack a few things before you go."

"What?" Isaac's eyes move now from the paper to meet hers. He might be regarding a stranger on the street who'd just asked him for the time.

"I don't want you back in this house, Isaac. Pack what you need for a few days. I'll have the rest shipped to you."

The paper he's holding slowly flattens onto the table. "What are you talking about?"

"It's over, Isaac. I'm going on without you."

She sees his incredulous look and finds it amusing. For days on end he acts as if he's alone in the house and now he seems completely confused by the prospect of actually *being* alone. She almost smiles.

Isaac leans toward her now, elbows on the table. "Have you lost your mind? Where are you going?"

"I'm not going anywhere. You're the one who's leaving."

He sits back into the chair. "You must have had a bad night," he says. He picks up the paper again and snaps the pages open. "Why don't you go back to bed?"

She tosses the earring across the table. "You should return this. It's expensive and I'm sure she's frantic about losing it."

He stands, picks up the earring, and drops it into his shirt pocket without once looking at it. She sees the color rise in his face. *Confirmation*, she thinks. As if any were required.

He looks at his watch. His frown deepens. He's uncomfortable. That suits her.

"Where am I supposed to go?"

"I don't care, you'll figure something out."

"What will you do?"

"What will *I* do? I'll do what I always have done." Sarah marvels at her clarity of thought, her calmness and the power she hears in her own voice. "The kids and I will be fine." She watches Isaac's eyes and can see him try to comprehend the abruptly altered vision of his own future.

"When did...how long have...?"

Sarah pours herself another cup of coffee and pulls a section of the paper out of the pile. She can feel him standing there. She feels his eyes on her and smells the nervous sweat that's slowly ruining his crisp white shirt. She pretends to read. She hears his cup shatter in the sink. The screen door slams shut and his rapid footsteps recede down the driveway.

She closes her eyes and looks hard into her new future. As she contemplates her first tentative step on the unfamiliar path ahead, a cautious smile begins to form.

MAY-DECEMBER
MARTIN DODD

You smile and call me sweet; it lifts my heart.
Your love inspires; my soul takes wing and flies.
It matters not that we are years apart;
It seems there is no limit to our skies.

With dreams, we race along on life's highway;
We pass the old and drive to find the new.
On top a crest, I gasp to seize the day;
Though we are one, I have more miles than you.

Now, hand in hand we stroll the lovers' path,
And as we turn our faces to the West,
My sun is lower (I can do the math).
I gather strength to give you all my best;
    A thing I fear I cannot guarantee,
      Because, my dear, I'm out of warranty.

NEW YEAR'S MORNING
Illia Thompson

Fog huddles close,
not ready to relinquish
early morning hold,
mirrors the mood,
of nearly to the minute
just one week ago
when fire melted lives
and structure into dust.

On my kitchen counter
sits portable white radio
almost two decades old.
The part that used to be
an electric can opener missing.
An appliance at half-mast.

I listen to opinions,
discussions,
charged feelings.
In touch with numbness,
a place in my heart opens.
Sorrow condenses into grief.

I prepare for the evening meal.
Matzo ball soup, started last night.
Traditional family holiday fare.
I roll heaping tablespoon-sized
balls, set them into boiling water,
watch them settle in the pot,
land immediately on the bottom.

Two dozen rest. One moves a bit.
And I play a hopeful game.
If that one does float first,
love will once more prevail.

A CHILDRENS' FURRY TALE

CAROL BROWN KAUFFMANN

Once upon a time there was a beautiful black and white tuxedoed cat named Charlie. Charlie lived in Pebble Beach with his humans who adored him and showered him with continual love and attention. He had the run of the house, but only of the house. When he was a little kitten he had lost his front claws, and his doctor had told him and his humans he must never go outside alone because he couldn't protect himself. (Actually Charlie *had* been out a couple of times when someone had accidentally left a door open, but he had always scampered back before anyone knew he was gone.)

One day as Charlie was gazing out the window at the flowers in the courtyard, he saw the largest, prettiest butterfly he had ever seen. He went to the screen door and stared at the Monarch butterfly from Pacific Grove. She had beautiful blue eyes, so he called her Ms. Blue. Charlie knew he was supposed to jump and catch the butterfly just like he would a bird. His mother had taught him these things when he was young. But he didn't want to catch or harm Ms. Blue. Instead, he longed to follow her as she glided from one flower to another.

Charlie moved closer and closer to the screen door and saw that it wasn't latched. He thought he could nudge it with his nose and maybe open it. No one was home to stop him.

Nudge, nudge.

The door moved a little.

Nudge, nudge, nudge.

The door opened for him.

He flattened himself and squeezed through the narrow opening.

Ms. Blue saw Charlie and knew right away he meant her no harm. "Hi, Charlie! It is a beautiful day! Are you coming out to play?" she asked.

Charlie stood as tall as he could and stretched to greet Ms. Blue. "I want to follow you and see where you live in this beautiful outside world," Charlie replied.

"You don't have to follow me, Charlie. I can do something even better," Ms. Blue offered. She opened her wings as wide as they would spread. "Hop on, Charlie, and I will fly you to my habitat."

Off they went. Ms. Blue flew straight towards the Butterfly Sanctuary in Pacific Grove. Charlie was mesmerized. Ms. Blue didn't have to follow roads or paths the way humans did. She didn't even need a car. She glided effortlessly through the air. She landed on the ground in the sanctuary, and Charlie got off.

He couldn't believe his eyes or his ears. He had never *seen* so many butterflies. Black, gold, red, yellow. Each one was more beautiful than the one before it. The quiet flutter of their wings was pleasing to his ears. Their wings played soft soothing music, the kind his ears liked. Humans were so loud. If humans had cat hearing, they would tone everything down.

Charlie walked and talked with the butterflies. He spent hours and hours with them.

Soon the sun started to go down. The butterflies were all getting sleepy and folding their wings for the night. With their wings folded, Charlie could not tell one butterfly from another. Even worse, he couldn't find Ms. Blue.

Suddenly he was scared. He had been gone much too long, and he was hungry. He didn't have any idea how to get home. He climbed the fence out of the sanctuary and started to walk in what he hoped was the direction of Pebble Beach. He knew he had been on some of these roads before, but only in a car. There were too many roads, and he was confused.

He knew he didn't have a tag on so if someone found him, they wouldn't know who he was or where he belonged. Darkness came. Charlie was crossing a street when he heard the screech of car tires. He jumped, using several of his nine lives. His heart was racing, and his hair stood up straight. He looked like a Halloween cat.

The car came to a stop. Charlie was afraid to move. A man got out of the car. Charlie recognized him immediately. It was Dr. Bill! Dr. Bill reached down and picked him up. "Charlie, is that you?" he asked. "What in the world are you doing out here? I almost ran over you! You look scared to death, and I'll bet your mom and dad are frantic." Charlie snuggled into Dr. Bill's arms and, feeling safe, he began to purr.

Dr. Bill drove Charlie home. There was a good deal of commotion in the house. All the lights were on, and all the doors were open. Dr. Bill carried him inside. It took quite awhile for things to get back to normal, but finally everyone went to bed.

Charlie went to the screen door where his adventure had begun. Outside he saw an odd looking creature flying around in a frenzy. It was Ms. Blue! She had been so worried about him that she borrowed some moonlight from the moon and sprinkled it on her wings so she could show Charlie the way home, but he had been too frightened to notice her.

Ms. Blue flew over to the nearest flower and folded her weary wings for the night. Charlie crawled into his bed and quickly fell asleep. Both were happy knowing they would be friends from afar forever.

KNIGHT AND DAY

MARTIN DODD

In worlds of dreams not bound by where or what,
Between sound sleep and wake, my heart gives rise
To hope and joy and love that wear disguise,
Such as a knight and queen in Camelot.
    Once more, I'm young and strong; my blood runs hot.
A dragon's slain, and lo, I gain the prize,
Her praise, "My knight, my love, my life," she sighs.
She is my Queen and I her Lancelot.
    But, dawn intrudes; I wake and she is gone.
The night's sweet victory soon fades away.
Bereft of sword and shield, I'm all alone.
In tears, I know a beast I cannot slay,
    For death could not be stopped or pushed aside,
    And so, my love, my Queen, grew sick and died.

THUNDERBIRD WRITERS GROUP: A POCKET OF CREATIVITY

Pebbles Writers Group is an eclectic collection of writers who bring varied skills, viewpoints and interests to their craft. The range of the members' expression can be glimpsed in the product of a recent group exercise: Imagine a coat, imagine a pocket in that coat, and imagine what's in the pocket in one hundred words or less. The Thunderbird Bookstore is not a coat, although it is warm and sort of wraps around you. Our little group, our little pocket of creativity, meets there. The following imaginings, pulled from that pocket, await you.

A POCKET LIFE
SHIRLEE ANDERSON

Her hand felt inside her right coat pocket. She blindly fingered two foil-covered teeth bleaching packets, a Kleenex, a lone button to a forgotten garment, a ticket stub to a San Francisco play, a restaurant receipt.

If someone found her now, dead on this beach, what would anyone make of her life?

"Always looking for self-improvement, no time to mend things, but time to go to a play, to eat a good meal."

"It's O.K.", she thought. Her pocket would be an O.K. summary of her life. Nothing to make a book of, just a "short story."

231

YARD DUTY COAT
JOY WARE

My grimy yard duty coat has hung in a school closet for years. Side seams and inside pockets are torn. When I emptied the pockets to take the coat to the cleaners, Band-Aids, a green pen with "Monte Carlo, 1996," a tardy slip from '95, lint-covered life-savers, a buzz top, three tiny wooden blocks, two dimes and a penny littered the table. There was even a note from my deceased husband, "Please stop for milk on the way home."

My biography could be written from the pockets of that tattered, red, yard duty coat.

ANGEL IN HER POCKET
MARTIN DODD

Birdie neared the top of the water tower. From the gathering below, someone yelled, "Don't jump!"

"I ain't jumping! I got business here!"

A man with a coiled rope on his shoulder began climbing the tower.

Birdie screamed, "Stay away. I'm taking an angel home," then muttered, "don't hassle me. I ain't going back, and I ain't taking no more pills."

The man kept climbing.

Birdie cocked her head. "What?" She reached into her pocket, removed her hand, and spoke to her cupped palm: "Okay." She smiled. "We'll fly away."

Some swore Birdie was laughing when she hit the ground.

A POCKETFULL OF TREASURES
LINDA GRANT

I removed my weathered, plaid jacket from its peg on our back porch. It was a friend. It kept me warm and housed my treasures: a pearl-handled pocketknife I'd found on a beach at Catalina Island; a house key discovered under a rose bush in our front yard. I'd spend hours imagining whose it might be. There was an Indian-head nickel dated 1927 and a winged-victory dime with my birth year inscribed. These storied treasures gave me much comfort.

I buttoned up my friend, stuck my hand in its right front pocket. Nothing! Absolutely nothing—except a hole!

WHITE SPORTS COAT
KEN JONES

Man, what happened to the good times? It's hell in here, relegated to the outskirts of the closet to rot unremembered. Once, I went to town, man! These days, I just hang loose here in the dark, suckin' up dust and feedin' hungry bugs. Then, my pockets held cool stuff like show tickets, valet parking stubs, a hot chick's number written on a Stork Club cocktail napkin. Now they're full of lint, scraps of paper, a half eaten roll of antacids. Man, I'd give anything to see the lights again. Hell, even a rummage sale sounds good.

A POCKET OF RESISTANCE
PETER HOSS

Imagine a sadistic law professor torturing a neophyte law student with the Socratic method.

"Do you intend to possess what is in your pockets?"

When the student says yes, the professor implicates him in a crime, because a miscreant has secretly planted cocaine in his pocket. When the student reverses his position and says no, the professor forces the student to admit he cannot drive because he does not intend to possess his car keys.

The student quits law school, prospers in construction, admonishes lawyers representing him: "Convince them that the contract means what I intend, not what it says."

POCKET MEMORY
HELEN OLSON

Susan and John met the frigid air as they left the restaurant. She snuggled into her wool collar and plunged her hands into her pockets. She touched an object that computed oddly in her mind. Susan pulled it into view — a packaged tampon.

The good sense of carrying this necessary female product yielded to the illogical — *they had just celebrated their 40th wedding anniversary*. John noted her odd expression, and she presented her find. They laughed, and laughed more, thinking how another woman, no doubt much younger than Susan, would soon be finding a pair of bifocals in her pocket.

CHOICES
ILLIA THOMPSON

Cleaning out the closet after her mother's death, Ellen remembers asking her, "Why don't you give away extra clothing?" Her mother's blue eyes sparkled, "I like to have choices."

Today, Ellen gathers the furs, checks pockets for spare change, cotton handkerchiefs, peppermints protected by cellophane. Inside a pocket in the mink coat, she finds an embossed business card: Marvin Fine, with a Washington address.

Ellen recalls, about ten years ago, Mother's regular Sunday phone call. "I'm having a great time. Traveling with a friend. Here's the hotel number in D.C." Yes, Mother, a respected widow, kept on making choices.

THE GOOD BOOK
HAROLD GRICE

Dust devils dance. A man, gunshot-killed, lies before me; his horse waits nearby.

What to do?

Town nearby, take him there.

Man's duster blindfolds the horse, gets him loaded. Easier to wear the duster than put it back on him. Hard, thick square in the chest pocket.

The killer charges, gun blazing, a slug slams me in the chest. On the ground, my gun in hand, I shoot him out of the saddle.

Why ain't I dead? Pull that heavy square from the chest pocket.

Over the tail end of a .44 caliber I see golden words: NEW TESTAMENT

Amen.

LIFE IS SHORT
PATRICIA MATUSZEWSKI

Pal blows out warm little snuffling breaths, reaches into my coat pocket and carefully removes the sugar cubes one by one, throws his head back to make sure he won't drop them, and munches contentedly. He checks again, no more sugar cubes.

Reluctantly, he ambles over to the salad course, a patch of shoulder-high Canadian thistles armored with thorns. He rolls his lips back in an odd grin-grimace over strong yellow-white teeth, and slowly and with infinite gentleness, nips off the first purple flower head. "Life is short, eat dessert first" applies to horses as well as people.

LOST & FOUND
GEORGIA A. HUBLEY

Sgt. Jasper Drake, a downtrodden war hero, watched his shack burn as he sat on the cold, damp ground. He held his head in blackened hands.

"Everything I owned, up in smoke," he groaned.

"I salvaged this," said Fire Chief Baker, throwing a worn camouflage jacket over Jasper's shoulders. "You're lucky you got out alive."

"But I have no place to go."

"Don't worry, we'll take you to a shelter."

Using his jacket for an extra blanket in the cold shelter, Jasper slipped his hands into the pockets, relieved as his left hand found the war medal still tucked inside.

THE JABBER WOCKET
MAY WALDROUP

There's a wocket in my pocket
it is green and it can scream
but it's just a pocket *dream*

Now this wocket has a sprocket
it is light and it can fight
but it's just a pocket fright

Then this wocket has a grocket
it can sing and have a fling
but it's just a pocket string

There's a *wocket* in my pocket
but it's just a jabber wocket

POCKAT
CAROL BROWN KAUFFMANN

She was walking home from Pacific Grove when she heard the familiar sound. She wanted to continue walking. The wind off the ocean penetrated her loosely woven coat. She reached inside her pocket. *Damn it! Empty.* No warm gloves.

The sound again! She couldn't go on. It came from the edge of the woods. She shined her flashlight in that direction, then walked to the gray kitten.

"Hello, little cat, you must be freezing."

The kitten meowed, moving towards her. She stroked its fur. The kitten began to purr.

"Okay, little one. You can warm up in my pocket."

IN HER POCKET
MARNIE SPERRY

A wadded up tissue, a couple of mints,
Half of a lozenge and twenty-three cents.

A green and blue cat's eye, a library card,
An old stick of gum that's gotten quite hard.

Two bobby pins and a ponytail band,
An unwrapped Band-Aid for a cut on her hand.

A bit of a dog bone, an old guitar pick,
A dried four-leaf clover, a Popsicle stick.

A Cracker Jacks ring, a roller skate key,
See, all of these things are quite special to she

Who's journeying now from tomboy to teen
And searching for self in the moments between.

ABOUT THE AUTHORS

GEORGIA A. HUBLEY retired after twenty years in financial management from Signetics/Philips Credit Union in Silicon Valley, and moved to the Central Coast in 1996. She is a charter member of the Pebbles Writers Group and the California Writers Club. She enjoys writing inspirational pieces, as well as nostalgia and fiction. Her work has appeared in *Chicken Soup for the Gardener's Soul*, *Chicken Soup for the Woman's Soul at Mid-Life*, *Good Old Days Magazine*, *Birds & Blooms Magazine*, *Story Circle Journal*, *Capper's*, and numerous newspapers. She has two grown sons. She resides with her husband in Carmel, CA. Contact her at GEOHUB@aol.com

JOY WARE lives in Carmel, teaches third graders and writes. Her published credits include essays in *Healing Ministry*, a national hospice-related journal. A feature article on elder care appears in the spring of 2003 issue of *The Handmaiden*, a publication of Consiliar Press. Other published work includes two short pieces: "Granny and the Case of Seagram's Seven" and "Shock of Recognition," both in the first Pebbles book.

KEN JONES moved to the Monterey Peninsula in March of 2001, after retiring from the Boeing Company. Southern California natives, he and his wife felt a growing attraction to the Central Coast over the years that became too powerful to resist during a visit in the fall of '99. Ken's working career involved a great deal of technical and business writing but he began writing for pleasure in 1985, focusing mainly on short story fiction. Ken is an active member of the California Writers Club as well as several other area writers groups. He and his wife Anne live in Pacific Grove with their deaf, one-eyed cat Lucky.

ILLIA **THOMPSON**, author of *Moments, Gracious Seasons,* and *Heartframes,* is also an award-winning poet and contributor to the press. She teaches Creative Writing, Memoirs and Poetry through Monterey Peninsula College and Carmel schools. Facilitator of private Journaling Days and Weekends as well as Intensive Evening Sessions, she honors the writing process at all levels and travels to share her workshops. Illia witnesses the arts as healing. Her paintings, displayed locally, offer another avenue of creativity. Illia serves on the Board of Directors of Donald Mathews' *Creative Edge.* She can be reached at P.O. Box 661, Carmel Valley, CA 93924 or illia99@aol.com.

LINDA **GRANT** earned her BA in Journalism from San Francisco State University and has worked for Bay Area newspapers as reporter and editor. She is taking a sabbatical from a second career in banking to write of her experiences as a child growing up in Big Sur during the late 1940s and early 1950s, prior to the introduction of telephones and electricity to the South Coast. Her poem, "Pacific Migration", is drawn from those years, when she sat at her family's kitchen table in their cottage at cliff's edge, watching the whales at play.

MARTIN **DODD**, a native of Atlanta, Georgia, moved to Salinas in 1965. He took creative writing at Hartnell College, winning their short story award in 1967. In 1968 he edited Hartnell's literary magazine, *The Spectrum.* Martin suspended his creative writing while he and his wife, Nancy, established and directed Sun Street Centers, a community-based agency providing addiction prevention and recovery services. Following his retirement and Nancy's death, both in 2000, he resumed creative writing. He joined the Pebbles Writers Group in January 2002.

240

PETER T. HOSS was born in Yosemite Valley, California and lived there the first eight years of his life. He has never adjusted to the outside world. After growing up in Palo Alto, California through high school, he attended Stanford and Cornell as an undergraduate, then Stanford Law School. After peacetime military duty in Vicenza, Italy (more like a paid vacation than a war) he moved to Salinas in 1962, practiced law for thirty-seven years, raised a family, and now enjoys writing after retiring (escaping might be a better term) from law practice. He has heard all the lawyer jokes known to mankind.

CAROL BROWN KAUFFMANN is a native of Atlanta, Georgia. She moved to California five years ago to pursue her writing career. She writes fiction, non-fiction, and poetry from her home in Pebble Beach. She co-authored *Juvenile Digest* in 1975 and *Passport to Education* in 1994. She was a frequent contributor to *Peachtree Papers* from 1982-98 (editor, 1987-88). From 1994-98, She interviewed Holocaust survivors as part of Steven Spielberg's Shoah Foundation, the results of which are being used worldwide for educational purposes. She is married and has a blended family that includes four grandchildren and a cat named Charlie, all frequent subjects of her writing.

HELEN OLSON Ever since she learned sentence structure, writing has been the "glue" that attached meaning to Helen's relationships and experiences. Her poems and essays explore the bittersweet realities of life. She hopes the writings she's contributed, teamed with her fervent belief in the benefit of laying one's thoughts on paper, will assist others to find their own meaning in life.

MAY **W**ALDROUP, a reader rather than a writer for the past thirty-two years, has enjoyed Carmel community life through the eyes of a bookstore owner. Born in Europe before WWII and leaving for the Far East thereafter, she liked neither reading nor writing. Fate decreed a new career (life begins at 40!) when she and husband John acquired The Thunderbird Bookshop in 1970. Reading became her accepted daily bread. She was instrumental in founding the Pebbles Writers Group. *Pebbles* and *The Barmaid, the Bean Counter and the Bungee Jumper* are resulting fruits of this group. As with a good dessert, she feels that these fruits are capable of enhancing the literary digestion of the reader.

PATRICIA **M**ATUSZEWSKI grew up on a ranch in Washington State and has lived in Mexico, Russia, Turkey, Princeton, NJ, Washington DC, and Pacific Grove, California. Pat has been a history teacher, a lecturer and administrator at Princeton University, and a grant writer for *National Geographic*. She is president of the Central Coast Writers Branch of the California Writers Club. Her publications include the script for a ten-part public television series, "New Jersey Legacy." Her short story, "Haint," was a winner in *The Monterey Herald's* 2002 fiction contest. She is at work on a mystery series set in Monterey County.

LYNDA **S**PERRY **J**ARDINE has written poetry for more than twenty years. The Pebbles Writers Group has provided the forum to further explore this avenue of expression. Also a harpist and painter, Lynda's aspiration as a poet is to bring her relationship with music and the visual arts to her writing. Other poems appear in *Pebbles*, the group's first book.

WALTER E. GOURLAY is a retired professor of Chinese history. He's been, among other things, a union organizer, journalist, editor and freelance writer for men's magazines, and house manager of a concert hall. He's writing his memoirs of the WWII years, including his Army service in North Africa and Italy, and doing research for an historical novel. He belongs to the National Writers' Union, the Fiction Writer's Workshop, the California Writers Club, and Veterans for Peace. A founding member of Fiction Writers of the Monterey Peninsula, he edited and contributed to their anthology, *Monterey Shorts*, (Thunderbird Press, 2002.) Two of his short stories also appeared in *Pebbles* (Thunderbird Press, 1999.)

MARNIE SPERRY has been a writer with the Pebbles Writers Group since its inception five years ago. She is working on a novel that's been bubbling about within her for three of those years and has written numerous short stories and poems, some of which were included in *Pebbles*, the group's first book, and in a book of poetry by Monterey Bay poets, *Plentitude of Poets*. She facilitates other writers in getting their books printed and looks forward to her own book on shelves in the near future.

HAROLD GRICE is a professional engineer with a practice in Salinas. He has written many technical reports but is now exploring fiction and biography loosely based on his own youth. His writings most often deal with character and the conflict of relationships. His work is laced with wit and humor. Belonging to the Pebbles Writers Group since its inception has provided a forum for reaching his current level of uninhibited development. He likes reading his works and enjoys hearing the work of others.

243